MADELEINE DRING

Her Music Her Life

Ro Hancock-Child

Micropress Music

Dedication

For Roger Lord

Acknowledgements
Special thanks to Courtney Kenny, Wanda Brister, Roger and Jenny Lord, and my own Michael who knows so much about music and computers and helps me with absolutely everything.

Second Edition
First published in 2000

Micropress Music
The Blue House
14 Brooksmead
Bognor Regis
West Sussex PO22 8AS
01243 827706

Second Edition text copyright Ro Hancock-Child 2009

ISBN 13: 978-0-9537893-2-0

All rights reserved. No part of this publication may be reproduced, stored in a retrieval system, or transmitted in any form or by any means, electronic, mechanical, photocopying, recording, or otherwise without the prior written permission of the publisher. This book may not be lent, resold, hired out or otherwise disposed of by way of trade in any form of binding or cover other than that in which it is published, without the prior consent of the publisher.

Printed and bound in Great Britain by:
CPI Antony Rowe
Chippenham
Wiltshire SN14 6LH

About the author

Ro (Rosemary) Hancock-Child (b.1957) studied piano with Margaret Howle, and read Music at Oxford (Lady Margaret Hall) with Susan Wollenberg and Stephen Banfield.

She taught Music and piano for 10 years at Keele University, where she met her husband, Michael, a pianist, singer and mathematician. Together they have recorded recitals of English song and piano music, including c.d.s of Roger Quilter, C.Armstrong Gibbs (taken on by Naxos), and Madeleine Dring.

Ro wrote the first appreciation of the life and songs of C.A.Gibbs, which was published by Thames. She has contributed to the *New Grove Dictionary of Music and Musicians*, and the *Dictionary of National Biography*.

She also composes piano music, and her Zodiac Prelude *Leo* is on the current examination syllabus for Trinity/Guildhall.

When not making a lot of Noise (musical or otherwise), Ro makes a glorious lot of Mess, and paints very brightly, and there is a growing following for her unusual art.

She lives with Michael, by the sea in Sussex, surrounded by orchids and very large amounts of deep blue glass.

Praise for the 2000 publication of *Madeleine Dring: her music, her life*

'The book is an amicably easy read – radiantly reflective of the special person [MD] whose subtly engaging smile illuminates [its] front cover .... The present desirable volume adds further to [Ro's] reputation as a communicative rather than an exclusive writer. Accessible writing satisfying both the specialist and the general reader'   **Rob Barnett**

'The book is an invaluable pioneer effort...I recommend it warmly'
Philip Scowcroft

Contents

Foreword from Roger Lord — v

First words from the author — vi

Prologue by Madeleine Dring — xii

Chapter 1: Biographical Sketch — 1

Chapter 2: Inspiration — 27

Chapter 3: Piano Music — 39

Chapter 4: Instrumental Music — 46

Chapter 5: Song — 52

Very Interesting Appendix (extracts from Dring diaries) — 67

Key to references in the text — 84

Bibliography — 85

Discography — 86

Catalogue of known Dring compositions — 93

Musical Quotations — 107

Index — 112

Foreword

Having, since her death in 1977, supplied various short biographical notes about my first wife, the composer Madeleine Dring, to musicians wishing to perform her music and enlighten their audiences, I realise now how inadequate these notes were.

When Ro Hancock-Child, the biographer of C Armstrong Gibbs (a composer whose music Madeleine much admired), made it clear some time ago that she would relish the opportunity to be Madeleine's biographer also, I was both relieved and happy.

This offer came about after I had asked Ro to transcribe Madeleine's youthful diaries (1935-1943), a task which greatly intrigued her. Since then she has spent a great deal of time in examining and correlating the music, letters and papers which have survived, sensing, I think, that she is investigating somebody who in many ways was very like herself. This has helped to make up for the fact that many of Madeleine's friends are no longer with us and so information, un-documented, has been hard to come by.

I think that Madeleine herself would like to be remembered for her songs and piano music, and for the pieces including oboe, which were mainly written for me to play. However, we do well to remember those special people who, as well as creating something to delight us, were *in themselves* objects of illumination, as if charged, like a waterfall, with positive energy, examples of that generosity of spirit which includes as well as the usual attributes of goodness and joy, the leaven of humour and a lively sense of the ridiculous.

I am very pleased that Ro gives some evidence of these qualities as well as the musical ones, in what she has written about Madeleine Dring, and I am deeply grateful to her.

Roger Lord

First words from Ro

Thankyou for reading this! To fill you in.

Back in 1992, Thames Publishing issued the first of its volumes of the songs of Madeleine Dring. My husband Michael (a baritone) and I (a pianist) were looking for new and interesting material to use in our recitals. We bought this publication and were immediately struck by the originality and wit of the music, and the beauty of the face in the photo on the cover. We failed to find any useful information on this intriguing lady composer, and asked Thames for help. I was put in touch with Roger Lord, Madeleine's widower. He had undertaken the daunting task of trying to promote his first wife's music, and was very pleased we were interested. He supplied me with armfuls of songs and piano pieces, many of them still in manuscript form. Their high quality was obvious, and we started to use them in our concert programmes, to which the reaction would invariably be 'What was *that* lovely piece? Never heard it before'.

We had already made a compact disc recording of songs by C. Armstrong Gibbs, which has found its way into the Naxos catalogue. We decided to try a whole disc of Dring. Our Malvern agent, Carol Holt, introduced us to the oboist Paul Arden-Taylor, who owns a recording business. We recruited soprano Luise Horrocks to sing some of the songs, and in 1994 produced *Love and Time* (named after Madeleine's song-cycle) which Paul took onto his Dinmore Records label.

Roger liked what we had done, and asked me to get involved further and transcribe Madeleine's teenage diaries, which turned out to be hilarious illustrated accounts of her ordeals at school, and her escapades at the Royal College of Music in London. Stephen Banfield wrote an account of her life for *The New Grove Dictionary of Women Composers*; *The New Dictionary of National Biography* commissioned a Dring article from Roger; Thames published more of her songs, and with this mounting interest in Madeleine, Roger decided, in 1998, that it was time to ask someone to write an appreciation of her life and work. He asked me. How lucky can a girl get!

There followed a very exciting time, during which Roger would produce cardboard boxes brimming with Dring memorabilia, gave me lists of famous and interesting people to contact, and entrusted me with many original manuscripts, which frightened me silly in case anything happened to them while they were in my care. I painstakingly located and catalogued as many Dring compositions as I could possibly find, played and sang my way through the whole lot, then set to work to write a concise biography and a commentary on what I considered to be her best pieces.

Help came from many sources. It quickly became clear that Madeleine had been very well-liked and was one hell of a character, known – yet never properly known – by many creative people, all of whom were keen to share their recollections of her with me. Given her popularity when she was alive, it seemed almost unbelievable that so few of her songs had been published. Michael and I wanted to find a way to issue some of the songs and piano pieces that I'd found in Roger's boxes. We set up a small publishing business, *Micropress*, in 2000; with funding from Roger I published the biography (*Madeleine Dring: her music, her life*); and then we started to print up some collections of Dring songs and piano music.

What has happened since then has been amazing. My book received warm reviews, and the initial print-run sold out in a very short time. People also bought the sheet music, and asked if we had any more. Yes, we did, and here it was, and we are still typing up new things that we find. Madeleine's *Idyll* for viola, expertly arranged by Roger for oboe and piano, was printed up by us and premiered on BBC Radio 3 by Nick Daniel. Dissertations and articles on Dring have been written, using my book as a springboard. The Internet is full of announcements and reviews of concerts which include Dring pieces. The Associated Board and Trinity/Guildhall currently offer about a dozen of her songs as examination pieces in the higher grades, alongside fine songs by her teachers Herbert Howells, and Vaughan Williams – she would have been well pleased with this. We started up a Madeleine Dring website (www.madeleinedring.com) which now gets very frequent visits. The bibliography and discography in my book became out of date very fast, and people are continually asking for further information. Things have definitely improved!

As there have been these great gains, so there have been losses. A number of the people who helped me so much have passed over, closing some chapters of history forever.

John Bishop (1931 – 2000). John started Thames Publishing in the 1960s, initially as a vehicle for the music of his wife, composer Betty Roe (b.1930). He soon took on board other music, particularly British music which he felt was being neglected, and he also started to publish books. He published my monograph on C. Armstrong Gibbs (*A Ballad-Maker, the life and songs of C.A.Gibbs*) in 1993, which opened many doors for me. John introduced me to the composer **Geoffrey Bush** (1920 – 1998) who was a pupil of John Ireland, and edited or arranged much of Ireland's music for publication. Geoffrey came to stay with us in Worcester. I'd previously asked John what Geoffrey was like, and he immediately answered 'incorruptible!' I said I'd see what I could do about *that*... Mr. Bush duly arrived with a car-load of apples for me, grudgingly played through a couple of his own songs, then spent the rest of the time in the bath! I never got the chance to corrupt him once.

John Bishop also wrote quite steamy poetry. He was a wonderful self-made man, and I miss him.

Michael Armstrong (1923 – 2000). Michael was an outstanding poet and painter. Madeleine knew him, and set some of his lovely verse to music *(4 Night Songs*, 1976). He fought in the Second World War and later moved to Jersey, where he ran a hotel and opened Jersey's first ever Indian restaurant, which was frequented by Gerald Durrell (Armstrong also worked for a time in Durrell's zoo).

Michael sent me all his published work and his correspondence with Madeleine, and I reciprocated by making a collage which included his poem *Resurrection*; he hung this above his bed, bless him. His extended poem *Memories from Underwater* is an extraordinary read, please take a long look.

Rose Hill (1914 – 2003) sang some of Madeleine's show-songs. She is best remembered for her role as Mme Fanny le Fan in the riotous TV series *'Allo 'Allo*.

Bill Blezard (1921 – 2003) was musical director to Noel Coward, Marlene Dietrich and Joyce Grenfell. For 20 years he composed Grenfell's songs and spoof operettas and could play the whole lot by memory, in whichever order she requested Bill supplied me with some interesting memories of Madeleine's theatre work.

Doris Crouch, Madeleine's medium friend from Streatham, who helped her interpret her dreams, passed on in 2009, aged 81.

My own parents, **Bill and Dorothy Child**, who gave me so very many musical opportunities, both died in 2006, leaving a vast chasm that can never be filled.

'Owever! as Madeleine used to say. I am very happy to report that - as far as I am currently aware - **Charlotte Mitchell,** Madeleine's partner-in-crime in revues, is still going strong; she was once (allegedly) a girlfriend of Peter Sellers. **Courtney Kenny** (b.1933) who enjoys Madeleine's music, continues to sing and accompany himself at the piano in cabaret, excelling in his interpretation of Noel Coward. The legendary **Andre Previn,** with whom Madeleine was photographed during her visit to Florida in the 1960s, has just celebrated his 80th birthday and is still much involved in music. **Prunella Scales** (b.1932, famous for her role as Sybil Fawlty in TV's *Fawlty Towers* with John Cleese) with whom Madeleine acted, continues her illustrious career.

Madeleine's son, **Jeremy Lord** (b.1950) has made a big name for himself as an inventor, and has founded The Colour Light Company. He says 'My work involves the creation and sequencing of light which changes colour, and of placing a singularity or multitude of changing colours within different forms to enliven, mesmerise and fascinate the observer'. His signature piece, *Chromawall,* took him around the world; now he accepts private and corporate commissions, and works with architects and artists including Martin Richman. It's difficult to describe in words what he does – it has to be seen to be appreciated – and it is quite stunning.

Madeleine's grandson, **Simon Lord,** is an unusual pop musician (current group is *The Black Ghosts*). He regards his grandmother as a 'music-hall satirist who was psychic'. One of his recent releases uses a synthesiser his father Jeremy invented in the 1970s, called the Lord *Skywave*, and incorporates music from Madeleine's instrumental trios, which is a daring move – have a listen yourself and see what you think.

And then of course there's **Roger Lord** himself, active as ever at 85, and totally willing to help me in any way he can with the make-over of this biography. He played oboe with the LSO for 33 years and is very famous in his own right, but you'd never know it from talking to him – he is engagingly modest, a real gentleman. He sends me chocolates for no other reason than he knows I like them, and he is a thoroughly generous soul. After losing Madeleine he married **Jenny Porcas**, a fine double-reed player like himself. Roger has been composing some rather beautiful songs lately, one of which (a setting of William Blake) won first prize in a competition run by the English Poetry and Song Society. He seems to like the idea of now being known as a 'Dorset composer', and recently had the great pleasure of attending a concert consisting entirely of his own music.

Connections

As I mentioned in my Author's Preface in 2000, it is my custom to circulate copies of my works-in-progress among critical friends, in order to obtain constructive comment. While working on the Dring book I found I was getting letter after letter which said 'Madeleine sounds exactly like you! Have you modelled yourself on her?' No, I hadn't; my role-model is concert pianist Valerie Tryon, who plays Ravel like an angel. I didn't know anything at all about Madeleine – that's why I was doing the research! - but the similarities between myself and Ms. Dring are undeniably there.

We are both Virgo (birth-dates a week apart). Both with the curse of perfect pitch, and a habit of linking musical pitches and keys with colours. Both skilful pianists and accompanists, with a love of short piano pieces and, especially, song. Desperately enamoured with all things to do with Rachmaninov. I compose music, too; short piano pieces for small hands. Both of us painters, and able wordsmiths. Both somewhat frightened by the world; total calm on the outside, pandemonium on the inside! Both electing to tackle our fears with relentless humour, and a gleefully irreverent attittude towards everyone and everything. I'm a rule-breaker par excellence, and so was she. And I haven't even started on the appalling hayfever, big nose, dreadful teeth, poor general health, total frustration with life's banalities (in MD's words, the 'supermarket and the sink')... Sadly I don't have her very long fingers (I have miniature hands, which makes piano-playing an uphill struggle) and I would have given *anything* to have her long blonde hair.

    I observed that Madeleine was an 'old soul', psychically gifted and spiritually very far ahead of me. Roger was well aware of his wife's gifts and wanted them documented, so I did so. I'm about as psychic as a lamp-post but, as luck would have it, my husband Michael is psychic himself and has been able to explain to me many things about Madeleine that I didn't understand. Michael psychometrically 'read' one of the Dring manuscripts, and I have put some of his results into the biography. He also says that, when I was transcribing Madeleine's diaries, he saw the figure of a small blonde woman standing next to the cabinet in which I had stored her books. Was she keeping a watchful eye on them, and on me?!

    When Madeleine was invited, in the 1970s, to give a series of talks for the Centre for Spiritual and Psychological Studies, she felt that she had been given a job to do which would oblige her to view life in a completely new and productive way, opening up fresh ways of thinking which thereafter could never be lost. Taking on the task of writing her biography did the same for me. I learned so much. I'm still learning.

    To be honest, I'm not altogether sure why I'm still here, when so many others equally worthy of a place in the world have gone, but I take heed of Richard Bach's words from his life-changing book, ***Illusions***:

> *Here is a test to find out whether your mission on earth is finished.*
> *If you are alive, it isn't.*

I take it, then, that my own mission is incomplete, and that continuing to research Madeleine Dring's life, and promote her music, is among the tasks that I am still required to do. It's no hardship: in fact, it's unalloyed pleasure! She put so much JOY into everything she did, it rubs off on you whenever you touch it, and carry on touching it I certainly will.

Ro Hancock-Child   July 2009

Any inaccuracies in the text are entirely my own responsibility, and if you would be kind enough to let me know what they are, I will put them right.

PROLOGUE

Ladies and most Gentle Men
Midsummer madness is here again!
This is the part where you can't drink and smoke
And we've lowered the lights, so you can't see the folk
That you missed upstairs and knew you should greet
Before sneaking down to pinch a good seat
(And I do refer to the chairs)
...

Sit back and relax – stub your fag on the floor
It's too late for the loo for we're bolting each door
To ensure your enjoyment,
Make sure that you stay
Now, one wave of me wand
And the show's under way!

So open the curtain and let there be light...

taken from Madeleine Dring's 'opening gambit'
for the Royal College of Music Union's "At Home"
in the Parry Opera Theatre, July 1973.

The Principal Boy

I'm a principal Boy – I am! – to end all princes,
How my audiences winces when I sing –
I'm a principal Boy, and I would be so happy
If I only could out-sing the King
I am dashing in fights, I am smashing in tights,
I am crashing from heights – But who's to know it? I hardly show it,
I'm a principal Boy and though my feet are aching
And my back is breaking – Be kind!
When I bat my eyes at you – Just give a clap or two.
I've got top billing And I'm *ever* so willing –
I'm a killing Principal Boy!

I stride about the stage With actions broad and free
I stand in streamline attitude, and sometimes spout a platitude,
I'm really awf'lly charming, With confidence alarming
And when I make my Entrance, How the chorus whoop and scream
You'd think I was the compere On a "Workers Playtime" scheme,
How they proclaim my little name Be it Jack, or Bobby Crusoe –
Someone's bound to pack a trousseau
For the Principal Boy – that's me! – A real top-liner,
Though my talent's minor, I'm a star!
I am luscious and coy, I may not be authentic,
But I'm simply *fren*tic to go far
My accent's still perfect While I'm off the stage
I only get cracking, when I'm in a rage
I'm a heck of a bore
And though my acting's tearful and my dancing's fearful – Who cares?
If you're enduring you will find me alluring,
I am loud and cheerful, I'm an eye and earful –
I'm the poor relation of civilisation,
I'm a bounding Principal, Quite invincible,
Blasted Principal Boy!

Words and music Madeleine Dring

Dring self-portrait with violin (1930s, taken from early diaries)

CHAPTER 1

Biographical Sketch

Music, the universal language, can express a pure and most potent form of truth, for it disarms the worldly personality by speaking directly to the soul.[C]

Madeleine Dring had a horror of biographical notes. She would doubtless have forbidden the production of a book such as this or, at the very least, done her mischievous best to sabotage the project. Once, while trying to write a dignified account of her life and work at the request of a music publisher, she suddenly found it all too much, and the little imp which bubbled permanently inside her burst out. The result?

> Madeleine Dring was born on the moon and can therefore claim to be a pure-bred lunatic. Arriving on a speck of cosmic dust she came face to face with the human race and has never really recovered. [N]

We may chuckle – for wouldn't many of us dearly love to flout convention and supply outrageous personal details, I know I would (and have!) – but beneath all this comedy lies darkness. Madeleine was well known for her humorous antics, but it is not generally appreciated that she used this flippancy and farce as a cloak of self-protection. She felt that she was very different in many respects from everyone around her, and this was a source of great discomfort.

Her outstanding musical abilities inevitably marked her out as unusual and special, but there was more to it than this. Her unfulfilled search to find her true path led her into the shadowy lands of parapsychology and spiritualism; she studied Jung and the interpretation of dreams, and counted several psychics and mediums among her close friends. She herself was acutely psychic, and spoke of her skill candidly, and with conviction. Such a gift enriched her creative endeavours, but it also gave her a much broader perspective on life: she unfortunately could see *too* clearly; she already knew things that most people barely ever come to understand. She found it very difficult to reconcile her wide view of existence with the sheer ordinariness and disagreeability of everyday living, and consequently her life was fraught with tension. The outlets for this were her composing and performing, and her irrepressible humour, which acted as a safety valve for the turmoil inside.

Early Life

Sharing a birthday (September 7) with Queen Elizabeth I, the equally strong-willed Madeleine Winefride Isabelle Dring was born in 1923, not in any lunar landscape, but at 66 Raleigh Road, Hornsey, London, 'dear London', as she observed in her diaries. Her father, Cecil John Dring (1883-1949), was an architect and surveyor, and her mother, Winefride Isabel, née Smith (1891-1968), came from a Scottish family. Madeleine's elder brother, Cecil, was born in 1918.

Her family life appears to have been very happy, the four of them operating as a unit for many things, holidaying together and enjoying a host of musical and leisure pursuits, 'playing together' in every way. Mrs Dring had a fine mezzo-soprano voice, and a programme from 1926 records her appearance at the same concert in Wood Green as Signorina Papacini from the London Coliseum. In an early sketch, the 12-year-old Madeleine drew her mother as a singing bird; Daddy, with splendid airborne moustache, is depicted with his 'cello. He could also acquit himself commendably at the keyboard, and was an able ventriloquist, with a male doll (like Archie Andrews). He had learned many entertainment skills in a First World War Concert Party, when not stretcher-bearing in the mud. Cecil Dring junior, portrayed by his sister in the guise of an African tribesman inspecting his timpani-cum-cooking-pot, played percussion in the family music-making, and Madeleine herself starred on violin and piano.

The Dring Family must have entertained, and been entertained, frequently, and their houses would have resounded with melody and with the laughter of friends, of whom there seem to have been a great number. It was 'Open House' after Mass on Sunday morning, and this often went on all day, with music playing a prominent role.

In her diaries of the 1930s Madeleine constantly rejoices in the daily comings-and-goings of (among countless others) the Duggans, the Masseys, the Chaplais, the Salgadoes, the Shepherds, the Rolfes, the Woollands, the Misses Feo, Flood, Everett and Lynch, Cullingford and Sanderson, Mrs King, Mrs Allchurch, Mrs Schwiller, Mrs Sterlini, all mingling with a steady stream of visiting aunties and uncles, both true relatives and adopted ones. The Drings' social circle was a wide and cosmopolitan one, and those were the days when conversation was sought after and relished, when people created their own imaginative entertainments, and the scourge of the television had not yet ousted the piano as the focal point of the drawing room.

Madeleine was privileged to have a quality piano on which to practise. She records an occasion when

> the Haymans and Geoffrey came in one evening to supper & to see the piano. Mr Hayman has seen it in Sir Phillip Sesoons himself (We were told it used to belong to him) He admired it immensly. It has a beautiful old painted case & a new Stienway inside. I have never played on anything so delightful. [D]

The 7-foot Steinway was bought at auction during the war. Originally the property of Baron F de Rothschild, Sir Philip Sassoon had it painted in the ornate Vernis Martin style, and the photo of it that I have seen (it's since been sold) is most impressive. Lucky girl!

Her immediate environment was very well suited to the development of musical skills and Madeleine, who had perfect pitch, flourished. Though heartily encouraged by her parents, she did not feel she had been 'pushed'; as she saw it, the opportunities were provided, she responded, and it was no surprise (though a great delight) when, after her Headmistress had happened to see a notice in an educational paper, Madeleine applied for a Junior Exhibition to the Royal College of Music (RCM) and was successful on her tenth birthday in 1933.

Appearance

A cutting of faded newsprint in Madeleine's scrapbook commemorates the achievement of 'GIRL VIOLINIST ... of St. Andrew's Catholic School, Streatham'. 'I must have been a cocky little devil'[D], she recalled. The girl in question poses very professionally in her photo, violin (a bit too big for her) expertly held aloft; white-socked and shiny-sandalled feet nicely balanced; short, white, lacy frock; blonde, curly, bob-cut hair. Very cute and very coy. And above all, very *small*. On first meeting her, one of her RCM tutors, Leslie Fly, remarked, 'I've got such a <u>little</u> girl to teach'[D], but at the same time he commented that, oddly, she did not seem to him like a child. The same ambivalence is apparent in other photographic portraits from her youth.

She has a most unusual, even strange, face, unlined and ostensibly that of a child, but at the same time intensely old in expression. The medium Doris Crouch, the Drings' neighbour in Streatham, considered Madeleine to be an 'old soul'. Madeleine herself believed firmly in reincarnation, so perhaps this current musical persona of hers was but the latest in a long sequence of past lives stretching back through the centuries.

Her trade-mark white-blonde hair she kept long all through her life, and her overall appearance was very pale: 'I practically disappear outside in strong light'.[H] Her most striking facial feature was her nose, large and distinctive, as is often the case with musicians. Her profile was frequently likened to that of a contemporary actress, Elizabeth Bergner, and Madeleine was highly amused when an examiner at the RCM paused, mid-piano-exam, to point out, yet again, the resemblance.

Upon reaching the 'glorious height' of about 5'2", she stopped growing. Conversing with Mr Tass, an RCM professor of monumental proportions, who took the same route to the College as Madeleine, was like 'talking to a mountain'[D]. Later in life, speaking of a trip to the USA, Madeleine recalled the crowded elevators, and how her tiny self was always jammed face-forwards against the much larger Americans: 'I've tasted quite a lot of gentlemen's suits!'[H]

She knew she was not strong. Regular bouts of childhood illness, including anaemia, influenza, rheumatism, liver attacks, deaf ear, scarlet fever and a 'breakdown' (she also attended hospital for a time for physiotherapy for her hollow back), put her at a disadvantage in some areas of musical study. At the RCM, Topliss Green felt that her singing progress was hampered by a not very powerful physique, and Lilian Gaskell, who took her for piano, noted that, even in her twenties, Madeleine was still limited at times by physical conditions.

As if in defiance of her lack of height, her fingers grew very long. 'She finds the excessive length of her hands and fingers difficult to manage', wrote Jewel Evans in 1939. However, Madeleine fought against her limitations, and went on to develop both a wide-ranging and flexible soprano voice and an enviable piano technique, becoming recognised as one of '*the* pianists' in her year. Although she identified herself chiefly with the violin when young, the piano became her main means of expression as a mature composer. Those elegant fingers allowed her to tackle 'heavenly' pieces by her 'darling Rachmaninov' before her friends could stretch even an octave, and she eventually realised that they were an asset:

> Up till now, I've rather resented my long tapering fingers ("long skinny hands" to quote Cecil) but when I watched Malcolm Sargent draw in a lovely tune from the 'cellos with just his little finger I think it's rather a good thing. You can express so much with them, not only with playing and conducting but also with acting and dancing, even just speaking ordinarily.[D]

Her teeth were not such a blessing. Their soft and crumbly texture meant that it was a case of 'Fourteen stoppings!' and countless sessions to be endured in the 'chamber of bliss untold' in the company of J V Cartwright Sutton, LDS, RGS Eng, where she always felt 'screwed up like the top E string of a violin'[D]. Not surprisingly, Madeleine got to know her dentist very well, and they talked about the 'higher arts'. He told her that filling her teeth was like doing sculpture. Her diaries record many days filled with pain, tears, blood and custard, and the consensus was that her nerves, and her feelings, were extra-sensitive. She idly wondered if what sort of a person you were had any effect on your teeth. We might wonder if what happened to her difficult teeth had any effect on her as a person – and on her health in general. Through it all she maintained her customary outer composure, but inside all was chaos. Writing to a penfriend, she confessed that: 'people get the impression that I am very calm and I often hate them for it'[H]. There was a great deal about Madeleine Dring that her friends and even her family were never permitted to see.

Early Musical Training

She attended the RCM just on Saturdays at first, and went to school in the week. She later won further scholarships which enabled her to study full-time at the RCM, and she maintained close links with the College for the rest of her life. She noted warmly that the RCM

> provided experience of such variety and richness that it has continued to spread its influence throughout my life. It formed a structure on which all events of real significance have been built, and I continue to learn from it by tracing the history of these happenings back to their source.[2]

Whenever Madeleine was questioned about her work, she invariably emphasised the importance of the all-round musical education she had received. She felt that the most stimulating and rewarding thing was the contact she had had with all the dedicated and lively people who taught her, including Freda Dinn and W H Reed (violin), Margaret Rubel (mime), Dorothea Aspinall and Betty Barne (piano) and Sir Percy Buck, Joan Trimble, Herbert Howells (1892-1983) and, very occasionally, Ralph Vaughan Williams (1872-1958)or Gordon Jacob for composition.

She brought her RCM teachers down to size in time-honoured fashion by the use of nicknames. Sir Hugh Allen she irreverently christened *Hudge*, E Angela Bull was dubbed *La Bull* or *Bullikins*, and Herbert Howells, with whom she had an ongoing love-hate relationship fuelled by his continual and infuriating habit of silencing pupils and teachers in practice rooms above, below and on either side of his chosen place of work, was *Erbie*, or simply *THAT MAN*. 'Coll', unlike school, was something that Madeleine preferred never to miss. 'I'm never absent as a rule – I love it far too much (funny what that will do)'[D].

Music-making at home continued in a lively manner, and she loved performing her own compositions. A hand-written programme for a concert at Orleans Lodge, Streatham (30th October 1940) gives a flavour of what was on offer – quite an ambitious recital for two teenagers. (Pamela Larkin was a childhood and student friend, and became Madeleine's bridesmaid in 1947.)

Piano Solo: (Pamela)	*Ballade in G minor* (Brahms)
Song: (Madeleine)	*Love's Philosophy* (Roger Quilter)
Violin Solo: (Madeleine)	*Romance* (M Dring)
Songs: (Pamela)	*Five Eyes* (Armstrong Gibbs) *One Morning oh! so early*
Piano Solo: (Madeleine)	*Suite: London Characters* (M Dring) *The Romantic – Hooligans – Man-about-town*
Piano Solo: (Pamela)	*Preludes in E flat and G min* (Rachmaninov)
Song: (Madeleine)	*Down and Out* (M Dring)
2-piano duet: (Madeleine & Pamela)	*Minuet, Tango* (M Dring)

NB   Roger Lord recently gave me some recordings Madeleine made in her twenties and thirties, and they show that she was an able and nifty pianist, with the ability to improvise at will. She also has a strong and clear singing voice, with a wide range and excellent diction. She takes what I would call a lot of 'liberties' with time and metre, and is a lawlessness unto herself in performance. I'm sure that she did not limit herself to one interpretation of a piece - her own, or anyone else's - but would experiment as the mood took her. How her accompanists managed to follow her in her songs, I can't imagine: no wonder she played mostly for herself - then she could do whatever she liked!

A Quick Eye for Detail

Madeleine's diaries of 1935-43 overflow with meticulously reported accounts of her College activities, and gossip about concerts and plays, exams and radio broadcasts, social encounters and music lessons. Above all she talked about her teachers and fellow students.

> People are interesting ... I don't think I ever stop studying or subconsciously trying to "place" or analize them.[D]

Her keen observations often took the form of cartoon-style line-drawings, many hundreds of which jostle in the margins of her notebooks, and crowd onto any spare piece of paper.

> I do the most ridiculous caricatures over anything that is rough...
> The sketches are perhaps a little cruel, only they're true.[D]

A tiny hardbacked book jammed with hilarious ink portraits is prefaced

> Any resemblance within to characters whether living or existing might well be the work of my subconscious mind, for which I disown all responsibility

(and well she might, for her 'subconscious mind' most definitely had a complete life of its own). Usually she drew 'types' rather than actual people. Occasionally someone would be specifically targeted, as in an unlikely rear view of Dr William Lloyd Webber (1914-1982, father of Andrew and Julian) at an orchestral rehearsal, prime candidate for a spot of pea-shooting.

Madeleine was especially fond of sketching eyes, silkily lashed beneath well-manicured brows. This may have come from her awareness of an "inner" or "third" eye which is present in psychically attuned individuals. Or maybe it had a dramatic link, stemming from her involvement in College productions where she was, interestingly, always cast as a witch or a fairy. The part she most enjoyed playing as a senior student was that of Oberon in *A Midsummer Night's Dream*. For one RCM play she recalls that

> my make-up was lovely – the most heavenly sinister slanting eyes and eyebrows – those eyebrows! Students tried to memorise how they were done. I startled an awful lot of people, even Miss Bull who burst out laughing. A good many people didn't recognise me, and I was told I looked glamorous and should wear them every day. I'm afraid I should get a bad name if I did, they made me look horribly vampy – but it just shows what a bit of grease-paint will do.[D]

She also had the delectable habit of giving people "the creeps" with her eyes. She was repeatedly told *not* to show the whites, *not* to lift one eyebrow, and *not* to look so wicked (one teacher at school called this her 'Come Hither' look).

In spite of her protestations to the contrary, there is every indication that she was indeed very well aware of the effect she was having on people. Her sense of drama was very strong, and she could perform with ease. She often turned her artistic wit onto herself, and penned vignettes of Madeleine at the dentists, the opera, at parties, with a headache, shaking with fear before a concert, and many more. These glorious self-portraits usually wear a sly grin or a demure expression, and leave the viewer with the distinct impression that this apparently shy young lady could be quite a handful if she so wished.

When she wasn't drawing, Madeleine created word-pictures instead, showing a remarkable depth of observation for a teenager. She was intrigued by people's appearance and mannerisms, and watched intently from the sidelines. After scrutinising the visiting soloists for a performance of the *Peasant Cantata* at the RCM she reported:

> The gentleman is the most bohemian attractive young man (I do get some adjectives dont I) a sort of study in black & white with an amusing sort of round face (something like Nina Martine),long black wavy hair, white shirt, black tie & a black pin-striped suit with baggy trousers that look like a skirt, but boy what a voice! He lay back in a chair right up on the platform a good bit of the time making gestures as he sang with his hands. The lady kept her hat on all the time.[D]

In fact, she made quite a lot of observations about quite a lot of young men who caught her sharp eye, at College, at the cinema, in the streets, even in the hospital where she went for treatment. Basil Rathbone pleased her for being a 'good looker' and Errol Flynn was 'such an original young man with dimples ... I like that blighter!'[D]

She also had an ear for accents, could turn on fluent Cockney at will, and poked fun at vocal affectation of any kind, as in the following account of the Headmistress of a school she visited:

> She looked awfully pretty, But oh, what a woman! I didn't think those kind of people existed apart from comic plays ...[she said our music] was delaightful! and how naice it was of us to come. [The Headmistress] scattering dazzling "welcome-little-strangers" smiles offered round some sustaining barlai sugah drops. They were stuck together so she said she was afraid she would have to make some loose with her fingah. Never maind, her hands were quaite clean. Whilst she spoke she quate – sorry quite often emmitted shrill, nervous but deffinately ... ladylike little bursts of high-pitched "how-are-we-enjoying-ourselves" laughter.[D]

Madeleine and her RCM friends fought to contain themselves at the time, but exploded in the car on the way back:

> We all went mad coming home, and screeched jazz and gave impersonations causing poor Miss Barne, who was driving, nearly to bash into a bus by the Albert Hall.[D]

She incorporated many of the characters she met into small playlets and short stories (mostly unfinished), and used social encounters as an inspiration for many of the lyrics of her humorous songs.

Musical Preferences

In her early diaries she freely criticised everything she heard and played. When only twelve, she attempted to copy a complex piece of Chopin from a recording, confirming Cecil Gray's discovery that a larger number of people owe their first authentic musical thrill to Chopin than to any other composer. Other musical 'thrills' came from Bruch, Prokofiev, Bax and, especially, Rachmaninov, on whose music she modelled her *Fantasy Sonata* for piano of 1937 or 1938. She was not fully satisfied by classical music, but at the same time cared little for the "Only a Rose" type of thing: it gave her 'the pip'. She astonished her dentist by telling him that she liked swing music; she liked 'good jazz', and she was enraptured by a performance of Milhaud's *Scaramouche*, exclaiming: '*this* – being played in the Royal College of

Music!"[D] A witty rumba (*Spring and Cauli*), for which she wrote music and lyrics, paints a amusing picture of the whole College which, overtaken by the joys of springtime, starts to swing – a fantasy she evidently cherished. Stuffiness in any area goaded her into action. Seriousness would not do, neither would conformity. Both she and Mr Fly ridiculed the airs and graces of what they thought were the over-qualified, pretentious musicians they saw around them. These Mus. Bachs were to come in for lifelong scorn from Madeleine. Aided and abetted by Mr Fly, she rebelled against doing any 'academic' study in music, preferring to follow the more practically oriented path of composition and performance. She was still satirising poor old B.Mus's some 20 years later, as in her lyrics to her song ***Don't** play your sonata tonight, Mister Humphries*. The bee in her bonnet never stopped buzzing.

An Original Mind

Her first manuscripts are miniatures, intended for her own use - short essays for keyboard or accompanied violin, resolutely diatonic but coloured by increasingly liberal use of 7ths and 9ths. The lure of 'fascinating rhythms' and the irresistible urge to write something 'truly modern' led her to experiment, in spite of words of warning from above:

> I've finished the piano piece on Mr Fly's little theme ... I said I hoped I'd excluded all 'squishy' chords from my piece He says I'm to keep off them for now. Just after he'd layed down the law the other week (he's done it before but those funny little chords keep slipping in), he was extemporising and played a beauty. He had to laugh and said "You've got <u>me</u> doing it now."[D]

Another new piece of hers was chastised because it 'wanders off into too many keys'. Nevertheless, those squishy chords seemed to keep flowing from her pen. Told that a new composer needs to be careful to woo publishers with non-controversial material, she took this advice temporarily on board, but looked eagerly forward to the day when she could express her own musical personality with impunity:

> I often think, that if I ever <u>do</u> make a hit with something really good and classical I'll turn round and write a red-hot swing number, just because it's never been done before, it would shock all the Dr's and Mus. Bachs, and it would show all the lowbrows that I'm not so far gone after all. Besides! the pure joy of it![D]

At the French convent Madeleine attended in the week (La Retraite, Clapham Park) she perceived herself to be victimised because of her musical ability. The music-mistress, in particular, gleefully watched out for the least demonstration of 'temperament' on Madeleine's part, and deliberately manufactured situations where she could belittle her pupil's talent in public. Madeleine was acutely aware of the gulf that existed between herself and her classmates, who she called '29 thoroughly unartistic children'[D], but she was adamant that the RCM was firmly against the production of precocious little virtuosi, and she certainly did not count herself as one of these. Regardless of what the staff thought, her class-mates, she knew, considered her to be 'shy, quiet, madly modest, and good'[D].

Friction at school did not abate, and so weekend Coll became a sanctuary, a place where she and her skills were accepted, appreciated and nourished. An endorsement of her talents came when she was chosen to play her own violin piece, *Romance*, in a live BBC broadcast from the RCM on 23 March 1939. The journalist in her devoted some 20 pages of notepad to this event. However, she still did not 'fit in'. In 1937, aged 14, she complained:

> Mummy says I am as old as some girls of sixteen... Other children (except a few at the Coll) bore me & I don't seem happy in conversation with grown ups unless I'm delving into some fusty deep subject.[D]

At school she couldn't find any children she could really call her friends because

        a)   None of them seem musical

        b)   They are horribly contented and unambitious

        c)   They are very small minded[D]

She confided to her diary that she always felt so alone – but this is a price that often has to be paid for originality. Others also noticed that she was a 'one-off'. At the RCM her teachers acknowledged her outstanding musicality, and exhorted her to 'learn the language' and acquire a solid technique, but then had the grace to admit that she must find her own path. Lilian Gaskell wrote in 1941:

> Her gift is of an individual and also many faceted character which in some ways will have to find its own way and solution.

Also in 1941, her teacher Herbert Howells observed in his report (composition):

> One wonders how, when and where she does so much work....Naturally musical.

Three years later he concluded:

> Madeleine is lively-minded to a great degree. But she's not for the beaten-track ways.

He was proved to be right.

RCM Plays

Somewhere that Madeleine *did* feel at home was in her ongoing involvement with the RCM's Christmas plays.

> I love acting passionately. It's my one big outlet a year. It's always at the back of my mind as a comforter.[D]

The plays were the brainchild of E Angela Bull, who was in charge of the Junior Department. Ursula Gale, a former pupil, recalls Miss Bull's

> rapier-like wit and a delicious sense of the ridiculous ... and a gamin-like love of shocking people. She would mercilessly 'debunk' anything that seemed to her meretricious or insincere.

Given what we have already learned of Madeleine's propensity for gentle parody, perhaps Miss Bull taught her rather more than just musical and theatrical technique...

As revealed in a 1958 interview with *Good Housekeeping* magazine we learn that Miss Bull

> writes her plays herself, mainly on the train from Haslemere where she lives 'with thousands of cats', talks RCM Professors into composing her music at minimum royalties, coaxes unpaid help from friends 'who are earning their martyrs' crowns this way' and if she ends the season with anything in the kitty, blows it all and more on scenery and costumes for a new play next term.

The annual productions were fairy-tale in atmosphere, and specifically for children. Miss Bull provided the scripts, coached the cast, made all the costumes and produced the plays, first in the underground Parry Opera Theatre and, after 1945 (when she formed her own Cygnet Company), in the Rudolf Steiner Theatre. Madeleine made her mark with her capable acting and then, in 1941

> Bull asked me one startling Saturday to look at the Little Mermaid and see what I could do with it for her – if I didn't like it, look for another Andersen. I thanked her dazedly. She wanted a ballet-mime. Came home in a dream of delight and read it, read others, and pounced on The Nightingale – chinese... It all seemed a great honour.[D]

Of the 18-year-old Madeleine's music for what eventually became a play version of *The Emperor and the Nightingale* we have little, except for a percussion cadenza and a few small dances, but it is evident from letters that much work went into Madeleine's incidental music and adaptation of the story; she even contacted a Chinese poet to ask for verse, and provided coloured sketches of the costumes she wanted. Frequent negotiation took place between experienced producer and willing trainee, kindly guidance was offered, and praise given. Miss Bull took great pains to explain the essentials of dramatisation (a discipline in which she excelled), and she showed considerable sensitivity in her willingness to leave Madeleine in charge of proceedings for as long as possible before intervening.

Whether Madeleine had lasting memories of the 'silk magenta trousers with the elastic taken out at the ankles... [and] the legs narrowed' is not known, but Miss Bull's advice on tailoring the music to the abilities of the young orchestra was of enduring value, as can be seen in this passage from one of her letters to Madeleine:

> I doubt if we've got anyone who can do one difficult rhythm you've written for side drum. Keep in mind the material we have <u>actually</u> got, not professional standards. I do these plays and the music to be of help and enjoyment to the children, not to try and attain the impossible. So everything has to be fitted to idioms familiar to them and techniques possible to them. They can achieve perfection within their limits but not even mediocrity when they are aiming at idioms beyond their capacity and experience.

The *Musical Times* (Dec 1941) felt that Madeleine had 'showed most promising gifts as composer and producer' in her involvement with *The Emperor and the Nightingale* and reported that 'A large audience was rightly pleased and impressed by an enterprise so full of capable and original work.' More commissions for incidental music swiftly followed, and she worked in a variety of media, including stage, film, TV, radio and ballet. She also wrote educational music for children, and demonstrated a remarkable understanding of the requirements of small hands and developing techniques. Her success in both of these areas came directly from her contact with Miss Bull who, to Madeleine, was

> a unique and wonderful person. I think of her with love and gratitude. Appearing in her plays (and later writing music for them) gave me some of the happiest moments of my life. It was also invaluable experience for work that was to follow.[2a]

War Years; Marriage

In young Madeleine's mind, war and excruciating dental treatment fused themselves together into one jangling nightmare. After one particularly traumatic session at the surgery she poured out her grief in a garbled stream:

> Don't know how I got home. I was empty, the jaw ached, I couldn't speak or swallow, the evening was almost airless, war might come at any time, I'd have to go away with that purgatory of a school - what would happen to the others? Cecil would go in the army, my career looked like being ruined. Why must the pavement wobble? Poor Mr Chamberlain![D]

The tumult of feelings that overtook her when she realised that conflict was inevitable left her numb. There seemed to be no future, least of all a musical one.

'Owever (as she was fond of saying), all was not lost. London may have been under heavy attack, and Madeleine speaks breathlessly of a narrow escape from friendly aircraft fire, but otherwise life carried on as normally as was possible in the grim circumstances and – a great relief – her beloved Coll. remained open. The doughty Miss Bull issued a characteristically brisk statement to all RCM students, reminding evacuees of their top priority in a war situation:

> Will you try very earnestly to keep up your practice. If there are no facilities such as a piano, in your billet, will you bring this to the notice of your Head Master or Mistress.

Madeleine herself was not evacuated, and stayed on in London to complete her schooling. She showed great strength of character, and took the attitude that she must go 'on with the dance', however arduous it might be.

The early 1940s must have been a bitter-sweet time for her. Her brother Cecil had joined the Territorials, and was called for duty immediately war was declared. He was killed before Dunkirk. Herbert Howells, Madeleine's teacher, showed concern by becoming active in trying to recover information about Cecil through his war office connections; tragically Cecil was never found.

But during the war years another young man, a very musical one, came into her life. In 1942, aged 19, Madeleine met Roger Lord, who was a little younger than her, in a drama class. Lord, a superb oboist, held the Gilbert Cooper Scholarship at the RCM and was looking for an accompanist for his performance exam. The rest, as they say, is history! On 2 October 1945 the Daily Telegraph announced the engagement of Flying Officer Roger Frewen Lord RAF, son of Mr and Mrs Lord of Wensley House, Northallerton, Yorks, and Madeleine Winefride Dring, daughter of Mr and Mrs Dring, now of Orleans Lodge, Woodfield Avenue, Streatham. They married on 12 August 1947 at the Church of the English Martyrs, Streatham. Madeleine was resplendent in a Grecian-style dress of white moss crepe.

Roger's appointment as principal oboe player in the BBC Midland Light Orchestra took them to Birmingham in 1947. He was offered principal oboe in the Hallé but chose, in 1949, to return to live in the Dring family home in London and play 2nd oboe in the LPO for two more years. He was finally persuaded to join the London Symphony Orchestra in 1952, and there he remained for the rest of his long and illustrious career.

A son, Jeremy Roger, destined to be an inventor, was born to Roger and Madeleine in London, on 26 August 1950.

Madeleine's mother, Winifride, lived in the Lord household until her death in 1968, and her presence made it possible for Madeleine to compose during the day. Ray Holder, a fine pianist, sometimes called in to play through pieces that had just been completed. He remembers little Jeremy and Mum always being close by, as he and Madeleine played through the manuscripts. Wanda Brister reports that Dring occasionally asked him to play through her songs so that she could sing them without the distraction of accompanying herself – and so that she could sing standing up!

Increasing popularity

In her twenties, Madeleine's music began to reach a much wider audience. In 1947 she wrote a score for a BBC TV revue, *Waiting for ITMA*, in which she took part, and she contributed music to a Dan Aitken play, *Somebody's Murdered Uncle*, which was broadcast on the Home Service. Lengnick published a fistful of her piano pieces in 1948, and recitalists began to include Dring works as the 'modern' component in their London concert programmes.

Pianist Kathleen Cooper premièred *Prelude and Toccata* and (with Dorothea Vincent) the *Tarantelle* for two pianos. A review of their performance called the *Tarantelle* a 'novelty', and a critic writing for the RCM magazine gave praise, then remarked that it was 'not too difficult technically'. This is a point worth noting. Much of Madeleine's music sounds quite complex, but an examination of the score usually discloses her clever knack of obtaining maximum aural effect for minimum technical effort; perhaps this was a legacy of her work with the children at the RCM. A pianist reviewing her *Fantasy Sonata* for *Musical Opinion* was pleasantly surprised by what he found:

> This has the decided advantage of being the easiest modern sonata I have come across. Easy in every way. Indeed, to one who always opens a new piano sonata with some trepidation its unashamed romanticism, simple construction and its almost Rachmaninovian freneticism was at first somewhat puzzling – and afterwards very refreshing.

He, too, went on to talk about the sonata's 'novelty' value. Why was Madeleine's music perceived as novel at this time? Part of the appeal may have been her femininity: women composers are still very much in the minority, and in the 1940s and 1950s a successful female musician was a rarity. Even fewer women wrote music than performed it, so Madeleine's curiosity value would have been high. However, her music was evidently making a significant impact in its own right, and it seems to have been the very individual character of her musical language that caught people's attention. She used a powerful tool, one that very few composers have handled successfully – humour.

Humour, Wit and Satire

'Composer is a wit' shouts a press report of a 1951 recital featuring Madeleine's *Festival Scherzo* for piano and strings, which she gave the engaging subtitle *Nights in the Gardens of Battersea*. According to one report, the 'racy high spirits' of this 'lively romp' were achieved by 'a kind of moto perpetuo full of the unexpected in matters of key and rhythm.' Moreover, her style 'seemed to have something of Eric Coates, something of Alan Rawsthorne.' The critic was impressed: 'Hooray for such a bridge between the Light and the Third!' In other words, here was music that was accessible to both highbrows and lowbrows, scholars and amateurs; it occupied a middle ground. It spoke eloquently to those aforementioned Mus. Bach's, who could not fail to notice and admire its technical brilliance, but it also included a strongly popular element. This music unashamedly and unrepentantly *enjoys* itself.

Madeleine believed that music 'opens the doors of the sky'. Her compositions are extraordinarily effective generators of light, and lightness of spirit. She was a very positive person, and felt a need to take an active part in putting what she considered to be the good things back into life, joy being paramount among them:

> Joy is something so special because it makes us young again, removing, if only for a few moments, all that unnecessary luggage we normally carry about.[C]

She felt that humour is a valuable cleansing agent: 'You cannot have a good laugh and be pompous at the same time.'[C] Occasionally she indulged in glorious farce, writing deliberately 'wrong' notes, comical figurations, rhythmical hiccups (as in her song *What I fancy, I approve*, see p.110), but most of the time she incorporated humour into her work in a more subtle way. Her musical tastes were many and varied, and she was attracted by widely differing styles, including Caribbean dances, French café music, Renaissance and Tudor dance music, modern jazz ... She took what she wanted from each, added something of herself to the mix, and produced a sound that is inimitably hers. Co-existing with the gaiety and the glee, however, was a capacity for evoking the bleakest of emotions; if we set side by side the *Polka* for piano and the song *I feed a flame* (from *Love and Time*) we can begin to appreciate the breadth of musical expression of which she was capable.

Not all composers' personalities are apparent in the music they write, but there is a great deal of Madeleine in hers. Michael Armstrong, whose poetry she set, told the author that he and Madeleine

> laughed a lot ... [but] at times she wrote that ... her life was in turmoil – 'Welcome to the Mad house' she once wrote to me. I think she liked to give the impression of someone a bit zany and featherbrained when in fact she was really a serious and deep thinking lady.

Hers may have been a wit born of despair, a cover-up for the apartness she felt from the people around her, but it served her well. She was able to put her comic talent to magnificent use in her involvement in a series of Intimate Revues devised by Laurier Lister, namely *Airs on a Shoestring* (1953), *Pay the Piper* (1954), *From Here and There* (1955) and *Fresh Airs* (1955/6). These immensely well-received productions consisted of a plethora of short song-and-dance items (contributed by an army of authors and composers) which were launched at the audience at the speed of light. Most of the turns were gently (and sometimes not so gently) satirical, with the result that bubbles were pricked, inflated reputations deflated and fashions guyed. Having seen *Airs on a Shoestring* at the Royal Court Theatre, London, Stephen Williams wrote that

> it is all gleefully disrespectful and even the seemingly romantic numbers have a saving disgrace about them.

In his autobiography *Swann's Way*, Donald Swann, whose talents (alongside those of others such as Michael Flanders and Joyce Grenfell) were promoted in these revues, remembered Laurier Lister as

> one of the most illustrious impresarios with impeccable taste and a wonderful sense of the visual.

Lister was meticulous in his directing, and could be rather precious (he often wore white gloves in rehearsals), but he was courteous and helpful to young composers, and he gave Madeleine and many other aspiring musicians an invaluable opportunity to present their work to an eager audience in the context of a highly successful genre. Several of Madeleine's songs were included in each revue, and were performed to great acclaim by talented entertainers such as Max Adrian, Betty Marsden, Rose Hill (a beautiful soprano from Sadlers Wells), and Moyra Frazer, ballerina extraordinaire, who managed to be both

Madeleine demonstrates her skill with the violin, which won her a Junior Exhibition at the Royal College of Music in 1933

With her brother Cecil, about 1926

Cecil and Madeleine Dring, about 1935

Madeleine, 1948

A Streatham portrait

'The Kensington Gores'
Madeleine Dring, Alan Rowlands, Margaret Rubel

Madeleine, with husband Roger
Lord and son Jeremy, 1953

Madeleine performing
in the 1950s

supremely elegant and hopelessly funny. Madeleine collaborated with lyricist Charlotte Mitchell on many occasions, and between them they concocted pricelessly funny numbers, lampooning social pretensions, in which they say those waspish things we have all wanted to say ourselves, but never quite found the courage.

Madeleine's satirical songs sneaked their wicked way into other musical gatherings too, for instance the annual Union at Home concerts at the RCM, where she regularly participated as pianist, singer of her own compositions, and commère. These events were in two distinct parts, serious pieces being sampled first and then, recalls Frank Merrick, 'the fooling which concluded the proceedings accorded with a long established tradition.' Madeleine showed herself to be a master of pastiche in an eclectic mixture of styles, fearlessly sending up her old teachers and colleagues. In company with a multitude of famous musicians, actors and journalists, she also took part in charity events such as the Green Room Rags, and concerts for April Fool's Day, where the printed programmes, themselves highly amusing, threatened performances of 'odd items ... and many intriguing and obsolete works'. Among them, in 1958, was Dorothy Pennyman's *Yorkshire Symphony*, in which Madeleine gave a spirited performance as leader of the Saucepan Lids.

Something she particularly enjoyed was her membership of the *Kensington Gores*, a Victorian-style songs-and-piano trio, which consisted on some occasions of Margaret (Peggy) Rubel, drama teacher at the RCM, who played Mrs Kensington-Gore; Alan Rowlands, her beloved son; and Madeleine, her not-so-beloved daughter-in-law! Margaret had a fine collection of period costumes which they plundered for their appearances on stage, radio and TV. Madeleine also had a happy association with the Players' Theatre, both as actress and composer. She appeared in an elegant revival of a Victorian pantomime, *Babes in the Wood*, and played alongside John Bailey and Prunella Scales in *The Silver King*, also a Victorian melodrama, adapted by Maurice Browning. In 1958 she contributed eight items to 'an agreeably highbrow hybrid', a revue entitled *Child's Play*, and was praised for her 'attractively off-beat music'.

Madeleine was also capable of writing high-quality 'serious' music, although she made it plain that, if it was serious, it was never 'serial'. In her teenage diaries she dreamed of doing some 'big orchestral stuff' but, finding she was nervous of orchestration (as was her mentor, Howells), she never did. She chose instead to write small-scale pieces – songs, short piano works, duets, instrumental trios. If she embarked upon an extended work, be it a dance-drama/opera (*The Fair Queen of Wu* (1951)) or a ballet (*The Real Princess* (1971)) she handled it in short sections, a bit at a time. The instrumental resources she selected are usually small, too, using a piano duet for her ballet music; and an imaginative and virtuoso solo piano part serves quite adequately as accompaniment to her one-act satirical opera, *Cupboard Love*, for soprano, baritone and (yes) corpse.

While plotting with fellow-conspirators on her revue material, she also produced some 60 beautifully crafted solo songs, which explore a rainbow of emotions. It is difficult to understand why so pitifully few of these glorious songs were published in her lifetime; several of the songs enjoyed concert performances by Madeleine herself and others, such as Richard Wood (whose small male-voice ensemble, 'Singers in Consort', originated in a World War 2 prison camp), but direct knowledge of the main body of these rewarding pieces was, until recently, limited almost entirely to a few people lucky enough to have manuscript copies. Thanks to the continuing efforts of Roger Lord, and Thames Publishing, the situation has now been largely put right.

Social Isolation

My reader would be forgiven for assuming that Madeleine was surrounded by friends of all kinds, and that her professional life and family circumstances were busy and rewarding. But there are many dark comments in her letters which suggest that all may not have been as well as it seemed. She appears to have found it very difficult to reconcile the demands of running a household with her need for space – physical and mental – in which to compose: 'I do my damndest to get a silent patch to myself every day. I find it difficult to go on if I don't.'[H] Moreover

> Living in different states of consciousness or vibration – one kind when you are doing the creative works and then changing gear in order to get back into practical living – this I find extraordinarily difficult. I am often unable to slow-down and this can cause one's metabolism to go berserk.[MA]

London, which in her youth had entranced her, in middle age was beginning to pall. Towards the end of her life she spoke of it as 'a huge city which is so full of cross-currents and much ugliness'. Despite the apparently unlimited opportunities for social contact in the capital, she complained that:

> I have so little social life in London – there are too many people, too many cars, too many concerts, too much strain – and things seem to cancel each other out.[H]

When she did have the chance to socialise, she often found it rather a chore:

> I do find it utterly exhausting trying to juggle with a cigarette, a handbag, a glass of wine, a plate, a knife and fork (that's six hands needed so far!) a stole and still retain the odd hand to be shaken.[H]

What comes across very strongly from her letters is her need for company (but only of people of similar outlook), and a deep desire for security and love; but alongside this was the requirement for solitude in which to work, and anyone intruding upon her personal territory was a major irritant. A contradiction such as this must have produced significant inner stresses.

In a somewhat unorthodox attempt to find out more about Madeleine's private feelings, I gave one of Madeleine's manuscripts, her song *The Cuckoo* (a delightful mock-Elizabethan setting of a wryly humorous poem), to my husband Michael, to hold – without telling him what it was. Michael is psychically gifted, and is an especially sensitive psychometrist. Psychometrists have the ability to sense information about cherished objects by touching them; for example, when held, a wedding ring will usually yield up images and emotions from the life of its wearer. Madeleine had some sensitivity of this nature herself – she told her American penfriend that she had found out many things about him from holding one of his letters – and she would not have been at all surprised that someone could equally well discover something personal about her, from touching her work. In his reading of *The Cuckoo,* Michael, working 'blind', correctly identified the item as a piece of music, and even stated the time-signature, then described several scenes which are unmistakably episodes from Madeleine's visits to the USA. But, to my surprise, the overriding feeling from this manuscript (in spite of the music's joyful style) was, he felt, of

> huge, unrelenting headaches, the sort that just won't go away and you can't do anything else when they come, and an overwhelming sense of loneliness.

The headaches may be related to the damage in her brain which took away her life so early, in 1977; and the loneliness? A clue to why she should have been lonely lies in a newspaper report from 1952. A concert to be given by Madeleine and Richard Wood is advertised, and it goes on to say that her husband,

> Roger Lord, who is frequently heard on the BBC, is flying to Canada this weekend with the Boyd Neel Orchestra for a two-months' tour beginning at Halifax, Nova Scotia, and covering the principal towns north of the Great Lakes as far as Ottawa, and then south of the Lakes to Philadelphia and New York.

Nearly 25 years later the situation was much the same: the front page of Madeleine's 1976 pocket diary bears a sad little list:

> Mar 7 - Apr 1 USA   May 10 - 13 Paris ... Aug 21 - 23 Spain, Sep 11 - 13 Flanders, Oct 1 - 8 Denmark,
>
> Oct 31 - Nov 18 Central America

Roger was away. He was an orchestral player, and orchestras tour the world. Even if finances had permitted, it was rare for families to be able to join the trips, and so they spent much time apart, something Madeleine found difficult to bear. She once told a penfriend:

> It's a wild and wet November night and I'm all by myself (not unusual, mop up the tears). Have to face being on my own a lot ... So I must dig in my toes and work. But I never get used to these [Roger's] tours, it makes all the difference to know someone is going to put their key in the door even if it's very late at night.

USA Visits

Sometimes, though, they were lucky. A huge collection of cuttings and photographs from American visits in the 1960s shows how much they appreciated the chance to travel as a family. According to US journalist Jean Yothers:

> the most travelled orchestra in the world, under the direction of 39-year-old André Previn, is in [Daytona Beach] for its fourth season as resident orchestra at the annual Florida International Music Festival ... London Symphony Orchestra proved to be music

lovers' cup of tea ... as the cream of Central Florida poured into Peabody Auditorium for the opening concert ... Luv, it was a glamorous exciting affair, equally as thrilling as seeing England's queen.

This was in 1969. The Brits braved temperatures in the high 90s and gave a series of what must have been sticky, but magnificent, concerts, and their hosts were captivated by what they heard. The previous year's tour was also thrilling for Madeleine because her new *Trio for flute, oboe and piano* was performed by Peter Lloyd, Roger Lord and André Previn himself.

Many transatlantic friendships were made, and contacts were maintained for years afterwards. Madeleine's compositional style was strongly influenced by what she heard on her travels, and some of her later pieces have an unmistakably American flavour, for example the song-set *Love and Time*. Her music seems to appeal strongly to the American ear, and one of the first companies to show an interest in recording Madeleine's work was Cambria, an enterprise partly run by Leigh Kaplan, concert-pianist and music teacher. Kaplan has done much to publicise Madeleine's music, and she was introduced to the Dring repertoire by Eugene Hemmer, an American musician and composer with whom Madeleine sustained a lively correspondence for the last decade of her (and his) life. In their colourful letters they chat happily and informally about all manner of musical and domestic concerns. Madeleine evidently felt that, in Hemmer, she had found a soul-mate: 'I am so glad you are a fellow nut-case!' she told him in 1976. She unselfconsciously shared with him her fears and frustrations, hopes and joys, and spoke of her growing dissatisfaction with the profession they were both in:

> I am writing some more songs and piano music but the mundane things of life do get in the way. I don't know why I'm writing them really, I wish I had a better plan of action. Let's start an "Encouragement for Drooping Composers" Club ... one needs to be in a special state to compose and have quite a lot of inner energy for music. And it's difficult to find people of one's kind who understand what a draining, intoxicating, exciting, infuriating, humbling business it is.

Humbling indeed. It may come as some surprise, given the magnitude and quality of her output, that Madeleine, in her forties, felt that her talent had, in the main, been wasted. She was mistaken, of course, but she went through a prolonged period of self-doubt and despair which knocked her off balance. We have seen that her musical career started very early in life, she tasted success relatively soon, and the future had seemed very promising. It came as a great blow when for some reason – probably little more than the fickleness of fashion – her particular brand of musical expression no longer seemed to suit contemporary taste. She felt that, in the 1960s and 1970s, music had taken on 'a neurotic and positively black quality that was never there before'[C], not even in the distant past. Areas of work which had once welcomed her had closed their doors, singers were now favouring lieder and opera, the BBC's requirements had changed, pandering to popular demand, and music publishing was in the doldrums. Madeleine refused to move with the new cold current of what she considered to be aurally incoherent music, and so the impression gained by those looking on, succinctly put by John Bishop, was that she 'fizzled out'.

Search for Truth

In fact, nothing could be more wrong. A time of difficulty proved to be the catalyst for a valuable journey of self-discovery. As Carolyn Heilbrun observes in her book *Writing a Woman's Life*, our most gifted children are often misfits, and Madeleine was no exception. Hugely creative souls have complicated lives, because the world is not quick to understand or recognise their worth; and the battle is not solely with their external circumstances: their most dangerous enemy can be their own self. For someone like Madeleine, for whom the pursuit of personal success was a permanent goal, to have her dreams compromised or, worse, unrealised, was distinctly unnerving. However, she believed that nobody is put on the earth without a sword with which to defend themselves, and *her* double-edged weapon was an obstinacy of purpose, and the willpower to turn an unpromising situation to her advantage. That is not to say that she found it easy, nor that she managed to complete the task. A search for truth is no guarantee of peace of mind, as Madeleine once reminded an audience, quoting the words of a priest: 'God is not a tranquilliser. Seeking Him may upset you terribly.'[C] In the same way, her own forward path was difficult and unsettling, and her life certainly did not end in a blaze of glory.

In the late 1960s she had already sensed the potential for personal growth. Writing to Hemmer she says that she has identified

> a golden opportunity for "Man, know thyself". I feel a great change of some kind is coming

and she later wrote of the imminence of a tremendous 'cosmic change'. Perhaps it was no coincidence that, in 1975, she was invited to give a lecture for the Centre for Spiritual and Psychological Studies in London. She initially took part in a large conference about the role of the Arts, both in life and spirit, and man's urgent need to find a new vision. The success of this venture led to further engagements, including 'a talk to a fairly formidable collection of people on "Living Creatively in the New Age" '[H]. She found this a real challenge:

> I have been given things to do that have required such a summoning and focusing of my forces that (with all the difficulties of daily living) I have had to keep very quiet and still[H]

and she came to realise that this work was a gift at exactly the time she had needed it:

> Preparing this opened up a sort of landslide inside me and became a way of life, that is, seeing and relating all things in relation to this vast subject ... I suppose one could call it a sort of spiritual exercise and the sifting of all the material became more important to me than the actual event.[H]

Her bookcases overflowed with works on fringe topics including parapsychology, philosophy, religion ('all kinds!'), extra-sensory perception, UFOs, astrology, writings by Rudolf Steiner and Jung ... She left no stone unturned in her preparation for these talks, and made copious notes in her customary pencil scribble (unintelligible except to the initiated). The jottings were then transferred into the simple hand-printing which was her 'careful' script. The chunky, thick-nibbed pen gives her work a solid and purposeful air. She also used this style for making fair copies of her music manuscripts: presenting her work in this way was a special ritual. The talks make remarkable reading. Unlike many composers, Madeleine did not publish her thoughts on the nature of music or compositional technique, so these painstakingly-crafted lecture notes with their mystical overtones are the closest we can come to an appreciation of her attitudes towards such intangibles as creativity and inspiration. The following chapter explores their content in greater detail.

Don't play your sonata tonight, Mister Humphries
For this night is so beautiful
Don't play your sonata tonight, Mister Humphries
For I'm not feeling dutiful
Oh I know that you are handsome
And you can play very well
But you know that I've had some!
And your music to me is just unrelieved HELL
So *don't* play your sonata tonight, Mister Humphries
And what's more don't explain it!
Oh don't make me a martyr tonight Mister Humphries
Won't you please once abstain
Let us capture Love's full rapture
Life could be so exciting
Without your damned writing
So *don't* play your sonata tonight, Mister Humphries, dear!

excerpt from **Don't Play Your Sonata Tonight, Mister Humphries**
(music and lyrics Madeleine Dring)

The cross-eyed ousle. This bird has a very nice nature but finds it difficult to focus on any one object. It only feels secure when standing in a puddle.

CHAPTER 2

Inspiration

As a small girl with a fairly strict religious upbringing I decided that atheists were lunatics but that there was hope for agnostics... I still tend to think that discrediting that which we cannot detect through our senses or prove by logical thought is closer to madness than admitting that there may be limitless possibilities that we do not know about.[N]

> Many people assume that going into the creative state means that you sink down onto a bed of roses. So you do – and you have to lie on the thorns![C]

Madeleine was frequently asked how she composed, and where her ideas and inspiration came from. As a child, she used to reply that she had written music for as long as she could remember, and she 'hadn't the faintest idea' how she did it; but she knew that composition was a gift from God, so 'what we must do is cultivate it and be thankful that we have got it.'[D]

When writing her talks for the Centre for Spiritual and Psychological Studies in her final years, she made a much fuller attempt to describe how and why she wrote music, and gave her audiences a tantalising, and sometimes poignant, glimpse of the turbulent world inhabited by the creative artist.

Psychic Awareness

Before we learn more about Madeleine's compositional strategies and musical ideologies, it is vital to understand that she had certain unusual abilities which deeply affected the manner in which she thought and wrote. Many highly creative people possess a heightened sensitivity which is the inspiration behind their artistic work. In addition to her musical talents, Madeleine had a strong psychic awareness which gave her access to other realities, other times and places. The world as perceived by our limited five senses was, for her, but a small part of what she knew to be a much greater whole.

It occurred to her quite early on that her musicianship might be a legacy from a former life; for instance, when Hemmer enquired at what age she had composed her *Fantasy Sonata* for piano, she replied:

> I wrote music ... long before I went to school. And it's nothing to do with being clever. I can only assume I must have lived before and brought through the memory.

She thought that some of her very vivid childhood experiences were memories of past lives, and she speculated that, as children, we are better able to recall previous existences because 'when we are new to the world, our [psychic sensitivity] has not yet been muffled'[C]. As we get older, our receptive channels can become clogged and our vision clouded, and our scepticism increases.

She believed in reincarnation, knowing that we are each on an eternal journey, and that when we are sent to earth it is to enable us to live for a while in a dimension that allows us to experience the passing of time. She chided those of us who pin 'age-tickets' on one another: 'As beings of spirit who inhabit these bodies we have no idea how old we are – not one of us.'[C] She knew that the spirit, or soul, or essence within us is neither young nor old – it simply "is".

Telepathy

As with many psychically aware individuals, Madeleine was strongly telepathic. She claimed that she invariably knew what her mother was thinking, she predicted the arrival of letters, talked with ghosts, and dreamed of events which subsequently took place. 'Magic or telepathy?' she enquired of poet Michael Armstrong, when she found that her selection of poems-to-set coincided with his own choice. A very striking example of her ability to tune in to others' experiences was witnessed by Michael Gough Matthews, a friend from the Royal College of Music. Michael was staying with Madeleine and Roger in Shaftesbury, where Roger still lives. While there, Michael had a disturbing dream in which, pursued by an angry crowd, he tripped and fell down a flight of stairs. At breakfast he recounted his nightmare; listening to him, Madeleine became

> very quiet and told me that she, too, had had an almost identical dream that same night. She, too, was in the middle of a riotous crowd ... and had seen a very old man pushed or falling

downstairs... On turning him over ... she realized that the dead man was me.

She had been telling Roger of this dream just before Michael joined them that morning.

Michael was not a 'very old man' at the time, and he harbours the uncomfortable thought that this was a prediction of his demise! An alternative explanation is that the dream was triggered by him falling out of the unfamiliar bed; whatever the cause or meaning of the dream, it cannot be denied that Madeleine co-experienced it.

Dreams

Madeleine believed that are 'spoken to' in our sleep and, therefore, dreams are of vital importance. She used to visit Doris Crouch, a Streatham neighbour and a medium/healer, to help her to read her dreams, since Madeleine was well versed in Jung. Madeleine also kept records of her own dreams in order to interpret them. Many of them seem to have been intensely colourful and filled with light. Sometimes she dreamed of beautiful harmonies, but she does not make any mention of ever having written down any of the music she heard while asleep. Her musical ideas came to her when she was awake – but in an 'altered state', a different level of consciousness from usual. She said that, in order to compose music (and, indeed, to listen to it effectively), we have to reach a 'higher awareness'. She felt that a creative person is one who is able to open up a channel between their ordinary mind and this higher state of perception. Paradoxically, the way to do this is not by effort and concentration, but by *not* trying –in effect, by 'letting go'.

Madeleine's words will be very familiar to practitioners of meditation, who make use of what is often called 'relaxed concentration', a state of mind and body where the usual busyness of thought and movement is stilled, and one's awareness is heightened. Exploring this theme, Madeleine gave a 1976 audience an eloquent account of How to Listen, first encouraging her listeners to go into a 'state of rest' and then instructing them to

> Allow [the] ordinary way of thought ... to drop away... music needs a special kind of attention but it is not the kind that requires the summoning and focusing of your forces. Rather let it be a thin stream, like smoke (or a pencil of light) that rises from between your eyes, up through the top of your head ... It can be helpful to

forget about the ears and absorb the music through this other channel.[C]

This approach may come as a revelation to those of us who 'listen hard' to music, straining our ears to catch the least nuance and felicitous phrase. There is every indication that Madeleine instinctively knew how to open this 'other channel'; it was the gateway for the music she wrote. Rather than inventing music herself, she felt that it came *to* her, and that she was tapping into some cosmic source. In order to 'hear' it she had to remain very still, 'like the animals do', put aside all extraneous emotion, and exercise the most delicate perception.

The Trials and Rewards of Being a Composer

'What does it feel like to be a composer?' her RCM teacher, Leslie Fly, once asked her. Madeleine told him that it 'felt funny'. 'Writing music', she later wrote, is a strange process. 'I think it is an activity of the soul ... For me, there is a definite feeling of awe attached to it'.

> Sometimes, when a piece starts to come it is like trying to tempt a little wild bird to eat from your hand; at other times you can be nearly knocked out by an energy that suddenly hurls itself upon you ... Always one has to step-back and let-go of one's usual feeling of "I am" in order to make its birth possible.[C]

The trouble with removing the 'armour of normality', and putting aside your 'safe and ordinary self' in order to be able to compose, is that it makes you vulnerable, especially on an emotional level. How right Mr Fly was when he teased Madeleine: 'you must be deeply emotional under that quiet, dry humour of yours.'[D] Her feelings were easily aroused, and all too easily hurt. She was also prey to waves of nostalgia, 'even for times I couldn't possibly have known. Anything from old magazines to a battered postcard can bring it on, and of course, music is the worst of all.'[H] She supposed that it is the lot of all creative people to have to endure a kind of 'incurable longing', and in her case the longing was for congenial spirits, people of her own kind, and they were few and far between. She often felt exhausted and very alone in her work:

> We do need someone on the same wave-length to talk to and oh! how at times we need reassurance and some kind of recognition – not in the way of fame, but of what we are inside.

Roger regularly told her that she did not see enough people (she spoke of her 'semi-hermit existence')

> but short of having the good fortune to live amongst kindred spirits, I don't know what one can do. I can't stand "women's chat" and I think "coffee mornings" would drive me up the wall.

She did try to socialise, and when circumstances were right she would open up and be very expansive, creative and witty. In new company she would make a remark to test the ground, but if this produced a blank response, that would be that: she would close down and just make polite conversation. Moreover, her composing often had an adverse physical effect on her:

> Have been writing songs suddenly – or rather being taken-over by the writing of them and getting an awful "tummy" as a result ... and couldn't sleep.[H]

She thought that most people do not realise that, when you are in the 'hypersensitive state' necessary for producing musical work, many things that support what she saw as 'normal' people are knocked away. She often felt that she was crawling on all fours when everyone else was cheerfully standing on two legs. She told Michael Armstrong that 'Keeping balanced (help!) while moving forward without too many back-slides is quite a challenge!'

In a curious way, though, her difficulties were a blessing. There is an old adage which asserts that great suffering is the father of great art. Madeleine endorsed this by saying that pain in some form is a troublesome, but necessary, element of the creative process. She explained to Michael:

> It seems to me that part of our [i.e. composers'] job is to use our pain and transmute it into some kind of understanding which will sharpen our perception and nourish our work – so in this way we don't waste nothink! [sic]

and later she wrote to him:

> You have a lovely sense of humour (transmutation of the pain again) ... Horrid and sometimes frightening though it seems – I have the feeling that our sufferings help us to reach towards truth – and when we surface from a bad time, we stand on fresh and firmer ground.

Through the wound that goes deep, or is repeatedly inflicted, she believed that the 'new child' – a work of art – can come forth.

Although composing was a 'desperately lonely occupation', it was also a privilege, and a bringer of joy. Madeleine felt that she was changed and strengthened by everything she wrote. Despite her intimate acquaintance with music, she found it almost impossible to define. She called music 'the most mysterious of all the arts', a language-without-words, an occult but universal language, a subtle yet potent force. It was strangely alive: speaking of a Purcell piece she observed that 'I even get the ... feeling that it is growing, like some immortal plant'.

> In the wealth of this invisible substance can be found every emotion man can feel – all despair, all longing, all passion and pain and aspiration.[C]

'Food for the spirit', she felt that great music is the result of inspiration from a higher level. When we experience truly inspired music, 'we are held, weightless, in another dimension.'[C] Madeleine believed that music's power lies in its ability to reach directly into *our* other dimension, our subconscious, bypassing our usual senses, and in so doing it has an unparalleled capacity for releasing the spirit. She always encouraged people to release themselves by dancing (in their mind, if their physical body is unable to do so): 'Moving one's body to music I consider to be a form of prayer and one of the most re-charging things I know.' She practised what she preached, and sometimes even indulged in a spot of 'dancing to the light of the moon' when visiting friends abroad. Ballet especially attracted her; she saw it as a form of 'limitless expression' and, for her, it had 'got the lot'.[C]

Attitude to Performance

Madeleine may not have had the physique to become a professional dancer, but she loved performing in many other disciplines – singing, playing, acting, speaking. In spite of her undoubted enjoyment, she never conquered her nerves: at a 1971 concert

> A frighteningly distinguished audience came in evening dress and I tried not to think about that side or I should have run away in terror.[H]

She also found performing very taxing, and once told Hemmer:

> I am in a strange state today because I had to play and sing before a gathering last night, lots of people packed into a very large room, so they were on top of one – and this is torture to me ... I feel rather jangled and fragile.

However, when in charge of her music, at least she could deliver it in the way she wanted. But she was often disappointed, and sometimes annoyed, by others' performances of her work. 'Do you get worked up when you listen to a public performance or broadcast of your music?' she asked fellow-composer Hemmer in 1972. 'I do, by the time it is over I have a wildly thumping heart and feel utterly vulnerable.' She quickly learned that a piece is not necessarily safe in someone else's hands. In her diary of about 1938, she wrote of a concert at the RCM in which Maurice Cohen, a fellow student and a fine, if somewhat idiosyncratic, pianist performed two of her recently written piano pieces, *Willows* and *Vagabond*. He caught the spirit of the music, but played rather too many 'Maurice notes' for her liking, prompting her outcry:

> It's hard for poor old composers when they hear things like an F slashed out at a climax instead of an E and have to sit up on the platform and look sweet – !^{D}

In her fifties she was still piqued by mistakes (as many perfectionist Virgos tend to be):

> I did get a hell of a shock when I heard [my] songs ... put up into those strange keys – it was quite uncalled-for ... [the pianist] also played many wrong notes in the last song and they messed about with the time.^{MA}

'I feel curiously naked when people listen to my music', she said; 'one is always hypersensitive about one's children-of-creation.'^{H} But another part of her realised that she could not control her music indefinitely: 'People perform from where they are in themselves and we can't all keep in step.'^{MA} Accordingly, she did her best to leave her work open to interpretation, and took care not to make it 'rigid with instruction'.

Those who did perform her music often failed to please because they approached the task too politely, too carefully. Roger Lord rightly observes that, in general, 'Musicians are so bad at being dramatic and tend to be over-self-conscious.' Many of Madeleine's pieces demand considerable emotional investment, and a degree of acting ability, to bring them properly alive. Of a pianist and accompanist attempting her *Three Shakespeare Songs* in the mid-1970s Madeleine reported that they were

> two very nice people – that was partly the trouble because they were too cocooned in their "niceness" to feel and interpret the bite in Shakespeare's words.[MA]

She, on the other hand, fully approved of 'letting the hair down', and her music asks you to abandon yourself to it; there is no room for inhibition. As she said, music's role is to 'unfetter the spirit', and nothing less will do.

A Misfit in a Frightening World

We learned earlier that Madeleine became increasingly dissatisfied with the world in which she lived. She found it difficult to find like-minded people with whom to mix, and she was not even at ease in the company of musicians who, she told Hemmer (acknowledging the irony of her remark), are 'a funny lot – look who's talking!' She viewed the 1960s and 1970s as a 'time of irresponsible chaos', and she was very concerned by the nature of much of the music that was being written, whether it was the 'raucous, sizzling pseudo-music' of the pop scene or 'that cerebral, cold-blooded stuff'[C] with which too many classically-oriented musicians were so preoccupied. She felt that warmth and tenderness were totally lacking in contemporary arts. 'Composers are channels', she said, 'and we are surrounded and permeated by strong forces, both light and dark, that are waiting to make use of us.'

> Those who are able to bring-through music should be aware of the damage that can be done to others when they launch their private nightmares and despair into the world.[C]

It is possible that she, on at least one occasion, felt herself to be a victim of those 'dark forces': she noted that 'there is a great art in knowing when you must switch-off'[H] and protect yourself from certain people, and she carefully assembled a list of instructions for (we assume) herself to follow should there be a threat from psychic attack. She also used prayer as a shield, often writing her own words. 'Prayer knows no boundaries', she wrote. 'God's work must always come first….Men are simply fellow-men to each other. To God, a man is a brother-god; know this and the light will always stream through you'.

Here is her own personal prayer, which she often used:

May I be given the opportunity to use my talents in the service of God.

May I be sufficiently in harmony in my whole being to carry this through diligently,

in inner peace and calm.

May each day and night nourish me and build strength so that this aim may be brought into fruition with joy.

Madeleine knew that she was eccentric. 'Life for me hardly ever follows a generally accepted path. I specialise in the unexpected.'[H] She was an onlooker, a misfit. For the 1976 RCM Union concert she wrote 'a sort of comedy lecture' for her own spot in this, appearing as a space visitor from the future, commenting on the civilisation of the planet Earth during the dark chaos of the 20th century. It was typical of her to use humour to disguise her feelings of isolation. Aware that other people might misunderstand her gifts and react inappropriately, she always took the initiative, and deftly defused potential problems by making fun of herself. As well as space-talk she often cast herself as a witch ('I am pouring masses of bats' blood into my cauldron and wishing you well with only the most exclusive spells'[H]) and she referred to herself as 'one strange lady', 'dotty' and 'truly nutty'. Her sanity, however, was never in question. Her husband, Roger, sandwiched between this brilliant woman and an equally psychic dachshund who regularly watched invisible people walking round their house, feels that he was the 'earthing side' of their circuit. Madeleine always felt less 'jumpy' once his key was in the lock, and he was home.

Creative Gifts

Although her life was never an easy ride, she was often richly rewarded by the knowledge that her music had touched hearts, and that her performances had lifted people out of themselves, if only for a short time. The purpose of her creative gifts was, she felt, to make contact with others; in fact, the whole theme of her life was a struggle to make, and maintain, such contact so that her understanding of 'the truth' could be conveyed to whoever was prepared to listen. The manner in which this message was conveyed was of less importance than the message itself. She wrote of a dream she had, in which she was asked which of her skills – acting, singing, speaking, composing – she considered the most significant, and she found herself saying 'They are all one,' each of them representing a different aspect of her creativity.

'No-one can tell another how to be creative', she said. 'It is God's way and they have to find it for themselves'.

Two months before she died in 1977, she was keeping notes in an orange exercise book. Here are some of her thoughts:

Jan 8th:

Accept what comes and you are master of the situation.

It is often through seemingly frivolous things that an important door is unlocked.

Open your gate and go out of your prison: you built it.

Jan 9th.

Learn to stand still inside yourself – then you can dance.

In the final year, Madeleine gave a persuasive account of what, for her, was the essence of a creative approach to life:

Living creatively would mean, in a metaphysical sense, removing all the hard lines of definition; feeling the ineffable mystery of things; living in a way that would open a door and let me into a new room – then having the joy of seeing that there is another door ahead ... bringing the awareness of these inner experiences back into outer life, making a new translation of it through them. Then, knowing by intuition when to put what one has at the service of others in the way that is acceptable to them.[C]

Given such awesome capability for spiritual insight, it is interesting that Madeleine wrote no overtly religious music, no church music, and set no sacred words. Although a Roman Catholic, who spoke of a belief in 'God', in many ways she was beyond 'organised' religion; her personal means of celebrating the marvels of creation was not by venerating any one particular icon or belief system, but by going straight to the very heart of things, rejoicing in Love in all of its forms; and, by using the 'great long ladder' of music to access a pure and most potent form of truth, she sought to make it possible for us all to 'pass through into the company of the Gods.'[C]

I've found the Proms

I used to sigh for Sinatra, I yearned to die for Ted Heath!
My flat foot was floogie, I was mad for Boogie Woogie
And I never stopped Jiving even to clean my teeth!
Jazz was my reason for living, Crooners my heroes of romance
I was deeply 'in the groove' And I'd no wish to move
So whoever went classical never stood a chance.
Then I heard about the Gala Ball
With Three Dance Bands at the Albert Hall!
I knew what to do - I joined the queue.
And thought it rather strange that I saw no-one that I knew.
On getting inside My eyes opened wide
Till I realised with a fright that I'd picked the wrong night!
We were standing packed so tight I couldn't leave without a fight
So Fate designed I should change my mind
For after that night it was plain
I should never be the same again.
'Cos I've found the Proms And I'll say they're wonderful
I've found the Proms And I'll say it's fun to feel
So full of music that's highbrow
That Culture is leaving its mark on my brow
I've got new friends We come willy nilly And when each items ends
We clap till we're silly -
To Boogie I'm waving 'good-bye' now that I've found the Proms
The men in the orchestra are cute as they can be –
I'm mad about a 'cellist –And I *think* he's noticed me
And June loves a bassoon And Win a violin
And Flo loves the whole of the L.S.O.
Each orchestra has its joys But we won't abuse it
'Cos in spite of the boys We still like the music
Oh you'll never know what a thrill is
Till you've queued for an hour to hear Cyril and Phyllis
I used to think Geraldo had vigour But Sir Malcolm has more –
And oh! What a figure -
I seem to be having it all ways
Now I've found my way around the fray at the proms.
In the office on a Monday they say "*Now* what's it going to be?
Are you spending tonight with Wagner? – or Mister Benjamin B?

When I've heard Rachmaninov I can't get back to earth
Might as well take the morning off For all my output's worth!
And Mozart makes me tender, And Schubert makes me glad,
And Tristan makes me want the sort of things Mum said were bad!
On the last night of the season, We have to let off steam
There's one of us who jumps And we *all* clap and scream
And the *shanties* accel and *accel* And we *get* in a bit of a *scrum*
And *some* of us faint as *well* But it's *all* good clean *fun*!
And when the platform's empty And the audience have drifted,
I stay there 'till they turn me out And I can't help feeling uplifted
'Cos I've found the proms Can't say what they mean to me
Jazz clubs and such Now aren't worth a bean to me
I'll never Jive at the Palais
When for much the same price I can gaze at the Halle
I've found the Proms My future's expanding
And it's all for the price of half-a-crown standing,
The wrong night, for me, was the right night When I found the proms.
Ooh! We're going in at last!
It's Tschaikowsky tonight! Number One in B flat,
Romeo and Juliet and Eileen Joyce
I've got to get up in front near the railings tonight –
'cos she doesn't half wear lovely perfume!
I never guessed such happiness would be mine At the Proms.
music and lyrics by Madeleine Dring

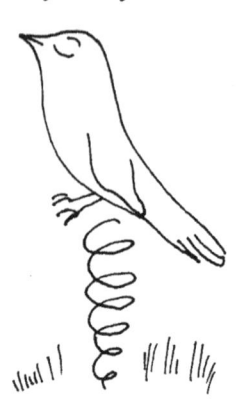

The leaping conumdrum. A mystery bird. It arrives in this country for one week (June 17-24) during which it jumps up and down in complete silence.

38

CHAPTER 3

Piano Music

Many people agree that there is room for all kinds of music in our lives... But when you put them to the test and play something less than highbrow, a nasty little puritan worm hatches out inside them. Symptoms are – a deepening of the colour (as though you had made an improper suggestion), glazing of the eyes, and one of those dreadful "I-am-waiting-for-something-better" smiles.[C]

Madeleine's music for piano is, in today's parlance, intensely 'user-friendly'. It fits so beautifully on all but the smallest of hands, because it was written by an able pianist who knew how to create the musical effects she wanted, without burdening the performer with needless technical difficulties. Once she had found her own piano style (after some experimentation in a grand, late 19th century manner) nothing is over-written, every little detail is made to count, and her pieces frequently sound very much harder to play than they actually are.

The piano is the thread which runs right through her musical work. She wrote for piano solo, piano duet, used the piano as accompaniment for her songs and solo instrumental pieces, wrote incidental piano music for a TV cartoon, composed a piano duet score to accompany a ballet ... She was completely at home with the piano, and had an enviable technique. She could play, by ear, almost anything she heard, transferring what was in her mind onto the keyboard with great ease. She claimed she was a poor sight-reader, but the evidence seems to contradict this; in all events, she must have been a pretty fine score-reader – her own manuscripts, with their thickets of accidentals, are visually very daunting, even when you are familiar with her harmonic language.

She wrote about a dozen works for the unusual combination of two pianos which, in the 1950s, was very fashionable. Nowadays two-piano recitals are uncommon, probably because of the difficulty of finding a venue with two compatible instruments, and also because of problems with co-ordination caused by poor visibility (it *is* possible to align the piano keyboards side by side, but this creates an unbalanced sound). Success depends on the performers having an excellent understanding of each other's musical intentions, and telepathy would come in very useful –this may well have been how Madeleine coped! Nevertheless, if a determined effort is made to surmount the inevitable obstacles, pieces such as the *Waltz Finale* are enormous fun, both to listen to, and to play.

Most of Madeleine's piano compositions are miniatures, and many of these are brimming with the spirit of Dance which she so loved. Some evoke the dance-styles of foreign lands (usually sunny ones) – Italy, France, the Caribbean – and a large group are directly modelled on traditional dance-forms such as the jig, minuet, hornpipe, waltz, polka, tango and rumba. Madeleine had a gift for pastiche in its very best sense; she was able to recreate the atmosphere of an epoch or a place while setting the piece very firmly in her own times. She spoke the musical languages of bygone eras and exotic locations with skill, and added some special ingredients of her own to create a style that is uniquely hers.

We have quite a few of her early manuscripts, written in her teens while she was a student at the Royal College of Music. Piano solos *Willows* and *Vagabond* were composed under the eagle eye of Leslie Fly in 1939, and have more than a hint of John Ireland about them. Madeleine's student works were often likened to those of Ireland and this surprised her, since she knew only a few of his pieces. Two other tiny essays, a *Waltz 'with apologies'*, presumably to Ravel (the opening bars are on p.109) and a jaunty *Polka*, are closer to the breezy style she exploited later on.

Like many a young composer, Madeleine had the urge to write an extended, Specifically-Designed-To-Impress composition, and the result was a *Fantasy Sonata* for piano (c.1938), fashionably presented in one movement and containing a good deal of 'Rachmaninovian freneticism', but unfortunately little emotional depth. Despite her grand intentions, I'm sorry but, as a piece of music, it just doesn't work. The sonata overflows with ideas (too many for its size), the abundant small sections don't mesh together convincingly, the ubiquitous fancy passage-work is devoid of significant content, and the multiple build-ups usually fall flat. That said, these 16 earnest pages demonstrate a most fecund imagination, and a familiarity with the keyboard that is quite astonishing, especially since she claimed that she conceived the piece while still at school. This must have impressed Lengnick who published the sonata in 1948, and such a vote of confidence in her work gave Madeleine the impetus to write more compositions for the piano, which had originally been her second instrument. Madeleine attempted to construct a sonata only once more, this time for two pianos (pub. 1951). Although the musical material in this later piece is more sophisticated than in the *Fantasy Sonata*, the design of the work is, again, less than satisfying. A reviewer for the *Musical Times* (March 1953) appreciated the 'well-sustained and poetic slow movement' but he found the rest of the sonata less personal and somewhat contrived, declaring that much of the material was 'suggestive of mechanism' and lacking in melodic invention. The message is clear. Madeleine's talent did not lie in writing long, structurally complex works, or in systematically developing one or two ideas in the time-honoured manner dictated by traditional musical formats. She preferred a much freer approach with the possibility of improvisation, and was far happier exploring a wealth of musical material in the context of short pieces such as dances and songs.

A much more successful work, one which sings and dances its carefree way through three action-packed movements, is the *Three Variations on Lilliburlero* (pub.1948). Madeleine adapted her incidental music to a play, *Apple-Pie Order*, to produce a lively two-piano piece in which the well-known Irish folk-tune is investigated from a variety of angles, and in every conceivable key. Shifts of tonality are often achieved in typical Dring fashion by virtue of landing on the 'wrong' note at the end of a phrase. The middle movement, marked 'Wallow' in the original play score, uses textures reminiscent of Poulenc's two-piano sonata, and the last movement of *Lilliburlero* indulges in several deeply jazzy moments, which provide colour and spice. Although the ear is continuously tickled and entertained, this music is not at all difficult to play. The air of complexity is an illusion created by the profusion of ideas. There is always such a *lot* going on, and this is true of much of Madeleine's music, even her slow pieces, which have a ceaseless inner motion and many notes to the bar.

The diminutive *Jig* (written by 1947) typifies Madeleine's ability to pack a great deal into a very small space. Nonchalant and unpredictable, it whistles and skips through a mere 48 bars of her favourite triplets and dotted quavers, prompting a *Musical Opinion* critic to describe it as a 'short and attractive little work, which, in its refusal to be ordinary ... reminds me of Percy Grainger – but with knobs on!'[5] Grainger was a celebrated non-conformist and original thinker who took great delight in surprising (and sometimes shocking) his listeners with musical practical jokes. In this sense he did share much with Madeleine, and he would greatly have approved of her *Polka* (pub. 1962), a pocket-sized caricature full of missed footings and wrong turnings. The opening trill demands the audience's attention and returns at intervals to check that we are still concentrating. The central section revels in a clownish bass melody, and overall the effect is 'cheerfully chirpy ... the harmonies move so rapidly as to give the whole an air of whimsy.' Indeed, it is often impossible to guess where Madeleine's tunes are going next, and she was also a very deft manipulator of rhythmic material, never missing an opportunity to ornament a plain phrase, endlessly alternating between 'straight' quavers, dotted ones, triplets and even friskier permutations, so that her music is perpetually streaming onward in a torrent of liquid sound.

A set of piano pieces which owe their character to an abundance of rhythmic elements is *Colour Suite* (pub. 1963). Each of the five movements resembles a mini-improvisation on a small jazzy motif, and is inspired by a particular hue. Madeleine had perfect pitch, and associated each note of the scale with a different colour. Unlike composers such as Scriabin and Rimsky Korsakov, she did not write down her own 'system' and, apparently, nobody thought to ask her what it was. It is not uncommon for musicians to 'see' colour in music (I do), but there is rarely much correlation between individuals' responses in this respect, and it is obviously a very personal thing. With *Colour Suite* we can match up five of Madeleine's pairs, namely: C major/red, D major/yellow, F major/brown, G minor/blue, A minor/pink. Elsewhere in some scribbled notes she marked down 'D flat/gold', and she said that minors had more grey in them, but the rest we shall never know. The pieces themselves are popular and attractive. Judyth Knight (*Dancing Times* magazine, 1972) recommended all five movements as excellent dance material. The seductive *Pink Minor* and easy-swinging *Yellow Hammers* have a Brubeck feel; *Red Glory*, brightly chordal, is like a Revivalist hymn tune and daringly relies on a single, repeated rhythm throughout; *Brown Study* begins in the manner of a traditional finger-exercise, but quickly shrugs off all such limitations and romps away. *Blue Air*, says Leigh Kaplan, evokes the image of a smoke-filled, half-deserted bar in an earlier decade, more Marlene Dietrich than American blues, and this is a style which Madeleine enjoyed. It appears again in the *Song of a Nightclub Proprietress* (a setting of words by Betjeman) and in a thoughtful piano piece, *Mazurka*. Both of these compositions are also in her 'blue' key of G minor.

The *Mazurka* is the first of a trio of solo piano pieces based on traditional dance forms. Snippets of the true mazurka rhythm break through in its middle section, but otherwise this is a very individual interpretation of its genre, as is the *Pavane*, whose only resemblance to its stately ancestor is in its measured tread; above a solemn 4-bar ground bass Madeleine constructs ever-more complex rhythmic and melodic devices, punctuated by a quirky cadential figure. The last piece, *Ländler*, takes the form of a whirling waltz whose metrical bass fights against the rhythm of the right hand part, setting up perilous cross-currents, and producing an exciting aural effect.

Another waltz of an entirely different character is *Valse Française*, which exists as a nostalgic and understated solo piano piece, and as a more elaborately dressed version for two pianos. The writing is elegant and enchanting. Madeleine's consistent 'lightness of touch and almost total avoidance of self-conscious profundity' (a compliment from Peter Frank) has unaccountably led some people to say that her music is insubstantial and light-weight. On their short-sighted scale of values, 'Tragic Symphony' scores more merit marks than 'joyful piano piece', and anything remotely humorous, or even simply good-humoured, is not regarded as 'proper' music. Now, much of Madeleine's work is a celebration of the good things in life. She did not approve of 'parading one's neuroses in public' as many composers choose to do, but instead deliberately sought out the fun, the gaiety and the glee – hence the sunshine of her *Caribbean Dance*, *West Indian Dance*, and *Danza Gaya*, the optimistic upsurging of *Spring* and *Spring Pastorale*, and the exhilarating energies of the *Tarantelle* and *Italian Dance*. She was not afraid to mark a piece 'Happy'. So it is regrettable that many minds still tend to judge the value of a composition in terms of its emotional depth, and devalue anything that is cheerful. The quality of Madeleine's optimistic music bears comparison with some of the most 'serious' compositions in the repertoire, and her craftsmanship is consistently fine.

The fact that she also wrote many so-called 'educational' pieces has also served, in some quarters, to diminish her standing as a composer of worth. What is not generally appreciated is that writing 'simplified' music for the use of learners is an exacting medium in which to work, and it is not a task that can be undertaken lightly. Indeed, Madeleine said she found it difficult to write music that was attractive while keeping within a limited technical range. She produced over 40 graded pieces to encourage and instruct new pianists, including *Twelve Pieces in the Form of Studies* (pub. 1966) and nine descriptive miniatures for the series *Five by Ten* (i.e. five albums, ten contributors) where her imaginative pieces sit comfortably beside those of contemporaries of the calibre of Edmund Rubbra, Malcolm Arnold and Elizabeth Maconchy. Two of Madeleine's pieces, *Nightfall* and *Spring*, are delicious little gems, fresh and appealing, proving beyond doubt that music's ability to please need not depend on it being difficult to play.

If Madeleine's piano writing is to be appreciated in full, reference must also be made to the piano accompaniments to her songs (see Chapter 5) which in many cases are more demanding than the works for piano alone. The song accompaniments also encompass a much wider emotional range than the piano pieces which, in comparison, have a more recreational feel. The piano parts in the two *Trios*, the piano accompaniment to her unpublished opera *Cupboard Love*, and the solo piano part in the *Festival Scherzo*, all illustrate how skilfully she wrote for keyboard. The piano-duet score to the ballet *The Real Princess* (based on the fairy-tale *The Princess and the Pea*) is particularly deftly written. In so many duets it is impossible to avoid collisions, or tangled fingers, but in Madeleine's score each player has the luxury of personal keyboard space. It is an uneven work, an amalgam of unremarkable ideas and flashes of genius. Outstandingly effective is the 'dream sequence' where the Princess is assailed by mosquitos, moths, bats and finally spectres, each with their own graphically drawn (and truly scary) musical motifs.

At Micropress we have published a selection of quirky Dring piano pieces whose manuscripts I rescued from Roger's boxes, and they are well worth a good look. *Prelude and Toccata* (1976) is a quality pair of pieces which would enhance any recital. The *Prelude* has a strong and almost seamless melody (unusual for Madeleine) which glides gracefully over subtly changing chords; its unruly *Toccata* partner is a crisp study in touch whose motivating force is an infuriating cackle, guaranteed to drive the neighbours to distraction while at the practising stage (I can vouch for this!), but highly impressive in concert, with its startling syncopations and uncompromising forward motion. *Moto Perpetuo* (a toccata in the style of a Bach prelude), *'Cuckoo' Dance* (modal and eccentric), wistful *Spring Pastorale,* joyful *Jubilate* (opening bars are on p.108*),* and *Times Change,* labelled as an experiment in 'swing' (a very successful one, and written out in purple ink), are all worthy of serious investigation.

Hammer on thumb, Or upset pins,
Indiscretion on two small gins,
Difference with baker, Hair won't curl
Man I love – seen with girl!
Tears at end of frightful day
Dropped two bricks and breakfast tray
They tell me it's good for my soul – Hooray!

For everything detestable is good for me
Everything detestable is best
If there's one man in the world I'd really like to meet
Then it's good for me to have to meet the rest!
And there's nothing like a really splendid struggle
With every kind of setback at the start
Except perhaps a gorgeous disappointment
With a broken promise and a broken heart
So that lots of bright optimistic people can
Ring you up and cheerfully suggest
That everything depressing
Is in the end a blessing
And everything detestable is best!

excerpt from ***Everything Detestable is Best***

lyrics by Charlotte Mitchell, music by Madeleine Dring

CHAPTER 4

Instrumental Music

It is most heartening to hear that one's music has made "contact"... to know that what you have expressed is "realised" and shared by another person is the only real reward ... (any artist) can have.[H]

Through her orchestral experience at the Royal College of Music, and her commissions to provide incidental music for Angela Bull's plays, Madeleine learned how to write for instrumental ensemble. She showed promise and originality in her orchestration, and an understanding of how to achieve interesting orchestral colour without making unreasonable demands on the players. However, she was always very anxious about orchestration and, in the 1940s, the piano, hitherto her second instrument, began to serve as her main means of musical expression. In fact, almost every piece she wrote involves the piano in some guise. With the piano she found she had a ready-made orchestra with which to accompany songs, instrumental solos, dramatic works, ballets, cartoons ... it was a reliable and convenient partner in whatever musical enterprise she undertook. Allied with the fact that she wrote mainly very short pieces (it is difficult to find any composition or movement of hers that takes more than five minutes to play), it becomes clear that we are not going to find symphonies or string quartets, overtures, or any other type of extended work in her output; instead, there are dances a-plenty, romances and idylls, reveries and impromptus, all of them charming and elegantly crafted, and technically within the reach of the talented (but not necessarily virtuosic) musician.

Madeleine's instrumental music is more effective in an intimate and informal setting, such as the Dring family concerts she knew as a child, than in an echoing concert hall. She wrote a great number of piano pieces, but only a few compositions for orchestral instruments, and most of these are solos with piano accompaniment. Among her early, unpublished, manuscripts are several short and stylish items for violin and piano, including a *Romance* in the Kreisler tradition, which she played at a radio broadcast from the RCM on 23 March 1939. She considered this to be a great honour, and the occasion is lovingly and extensively documented in her diary of that year.

After the death of her RCM violin tutor, W H Reed, she seems to have forsaken the violin completely. From her short residence in Birmingham come two pieces which feature other strings: the first is a *Tango* for solo 'cello, strings, woodwind, percussion and piano, written for Lance Bowen in 1948. It is an excellent tango, full of heat and passion and shimmering woodwind glissandi – but it is not a Dring tango; Madeleine has captured the style to perfection, but there is little of her own musical personality in it. The *Tango* for oboe (pub. 1983), even with its Bernstein accent, is a much more personal interpretation.

The *Idyll* for solo viola and piano for Hope Hamburg (also 1948) bears many more Dring hallmarks. In her favourite metre, 6/8, the *Idyll* is very similar in style to two of the solo piano pieces – *Spring* (from *Five by Ten*) and *Spring Pastorale*. Roger observed that spring, for Madeleine, always had a tinge of sadness mingled with its optimistic new growth and, in the same way, this viola piece is both hopeful yet wistful. Madeleine often spoke of an intense and inexplicable longing she constantly felt (which she assumed is something that all creative people have to endure) and the *Idyll* could be said to be a musical portrayal of this yearning feeling, which is crystallised in the chords of its opening bars. It is a gentle, hypnotic piece, almost a lullaby, tinted with modal harmonies and parallel chords. The viola line is deeply expressive, and even has a mini-cadenza at its most passionate point. Madeleine approached Lengnick with it, and was encouraged to submit her manuscript 'provided there is no nonsense with the rhythm' (which there is not), but for some unfathomable reason it failed to impress. It then had to wait some 50 years before Micropress published it. People who now pick up a copy say 'wow'! Roger made a lovely arrangement of it for oboe and piano, and Nick Daniel, oboist supreme, premièred it for us on BBC Radio 3. It has been beautifully recorded by the Quartz Ensemble, and I hope this piece will become very well-known and much played, because it is simply magical (opening bars p.107).

A string orchestra accompanies the solo piano in the *Festival Scherzo* (*Nights in the Gardens of Battersea*), providing a chattering backdrop to a frisky, non-stop keyboard caper, written to celebrate the Festival of Britain of 1951. This is another tiny work that packs a huge amount into its modest 140 bars; no sooner has it hit you in the face with its galloping antics than it is accelerating away in a mad dash to the finish. The piano writing is agile and economical, impressive but not at all difficult, and above all it is in the Dring tradition of Great Fun, both to hear, and to play.

Also humorous and warm-hearted is the *Trio for flute, oboe, and piano,* composed in 1968 for Musica da Camera. After several UK performances it was featured at the Florida International Music Festival, with André Previn at the piano. The three contrasting instruments are expertly blended, but the individuality of their respective characters is maintained throughout; the Poulenc-style accompaniment exploits the piano's percussive qualities, and the oboe and flute are given ample opportunity to show off their lyrical capabilities. The fine middle movement possesses 'that calm and tender quality of affirmation'[RL] found in so much of Madeleine's music. She had difficulty in finding suitable additional material to complement the beauty of her tune, and the manuscript of the central section of this movement was uncharacteristically rubbered-to-death before she was satisfied: a perfectionist to the core, nothing less than the best would ever do. The last movement is a hilarious spoof which takes as its target those empty 18th and 19th century pieces that are hell-bent on demonstrating every last detail of their performers' technical prowess. Based around a mock-serious theme (which owes much to Brahms' 4th) there is a considerable amount of hocketing and jockeying for position. In the midst of the tomfoolery there erupts a joint cadenza for oboe and flute; before anyone can win, however, their tussle is irritably curtailed by the piano which has become tired of being left out. This is Madeleine at her satirical best, combining the finest quality music with first-rate entertainment.

Being married to a world-class oboist meant that she had a head start when composing for double-reeds but, typically, she did not (as she could so easily have done) write finger-shatteringly difficult works. In their younger days, she and Roger appeared together in concert, often playing her compositions, but Roger's increasingly heavy load of orchestral work robbed them of the opportunity to function as a musical team. For oboe and piano she wrote five dances, three of which were later arranged for flute and piano (the oboe *Waltz* was reworked as *WIB Waltz,* for flautist WIlliam Bennett). Most distinctive are the *Polka* and the *Italian Dance,* a spiky Tarantella.

Oboe also plays a prominent role in the *Trio for oboe, bassoon and harpsichord*, an idiosyncratic combination of reedy resonances. From 1971, this is worlds apart from the *Trio for flute, oboe and piano*. Reactions to a first hearing of the 1971 *Trio* vary wildly. Letters I have received from musicians familiar with her work speak of it being 'endlessly inventive', 'difficult to grasp initially, but it really grows on you' and even 'music to go mad by'! The piece has many layers, and it can be approached from many angles, which is perhaps why people relate to it so differently. The Athenaeum Ensemble gave this *Trio* its Wigmore Hall première using harpsichord (for which it was conceived) but at later performances it was discovered that the keyboard writing was equally effective on piano, the themes coming through more strongly. The emphatic and declamatory opening movement is nominally a march, but its rapid time changes give it a restlessness which might explain why it is difficult for some listeners to settle into the work; on the other hand, the freedom with which the *March* is treated provides an engaging freshness which is intensified by the main theme's raised 4th (as in the song *Sister, awake* from the same period). The keyboard textures have a strong affinity with the piano writing of Geoffrey Bush, which also depends on headstrong scales and bold, rhythmic counterpoint for its intellectual appeal. *Dialogues*, the central movement, is an oasis of calm, spacious, uncluttered and untroubled; with all unessential details stripped away, the music has the composure and lucidity found in some of Holst's mystical song-settings. A tangle of musical 'seeds' adorns the cover of the manuscript of the final movement, and Madeleine threads these tiny motifs together in innumerable permutations to form a complex web which, in many ways, is an extended and fiercer version of the song *Upper Lambourne* (from the Betjeman set) – they are both in 5/8 and share melodies and keyboard figurations. The *Trio* also borrows the hammering fistfuls of piano notes which give the song *I feed a flame* such awesome momentum. A passage near the end is marked 'as bells', and other sections of the piece also explore the sonorities of church bells, particularly their clashes and sharp-edged reverberation. This late work epitomises the uncompromising and vigorous style with which Madeleine was absorbed in the 1970s. Not an easy piece to play or to experience, it richly repays close study, and is probably better understood and appreciated if acquaintance has first been made with some of her less challenging compositions.

Mention must be made of the *Three-Piece Suite* that is now being widely played and recorded. This started life as a *Suite for Harmonica and Piano;* obviously it was not going to be much performed as such, and Roger made an arrangement of it for oboe and piano, making some minor adjustments, adding expression marks and dynamics, changing the key of the central section, and giving titles to the movements. It works extremely well in its new incarnation, and the oboe supplies the 'bite' it needs. I have made a solo piano arrangement of the middle movement (*Romance*) and have kept it in the original key of C major, which I feel sings better than B flat; it has a gloriously easy-going American accent, and is just like a lazy walk in a sunny park.

TORCH SONG

Sometimes I get weary
Sometimes I get sad
Sometimes I'm just bleary
Others awful bad
But when your bank account I see,
I'm determined you were meant to be
The only man for me
But lately I fear our liaison is tending
To fail in a way you can't see
It's nothing to you but to me it's unending.
With each new sin I have loved you more
There's just one thing that I deplore:

Take me unawares, Kick me down the stairs
Deceive me and leave me on the brink!
But DARLING since you say you love me
Don't stop up the sink!
When I'm admired Tell me I look tired (Thanks)
Abuse me and trample on my mink!
But Baby if you want your honey
Don't stop up the sink!

After passion has reached the heights
Someone's gotta make a cuppa tea
Someone's gotta do the washing-up
That SOMEONE is me!

Slash me to bits
Make the Sunday headlines
Call me your niece and then wink!
But Darling if you want my deadline
[shakes head] um…um…
I'm jus' dead sick of dat ole plunger!!

Play to me on your recorder
[burst of *Sheep may safely graze*]
Read me your verse that never rhymes
But don't make me send for the plumber again
He comes at such very awkward times

Oh go and play bowls
Discuss your Operation
Read me the <u>whole</u> of Percy Scholes
But Darling for my full co-operation
Do just as you think
Pop drugs in my drink
But Don't stop up the sink.

Words and music Madeleine Dring

The get-ahead bird. It marches ever onwards and gazes ever upwards. Unfortunately it has lost most of its beak through constantly bumping into obstacles.

CHAPTER 5

Song

I think we learn most vividly through all forms of love... if we love deeply, we animate the soul... if we love possessively and demandingly, we love with the ego – and that is the most treacherous horse to ride... the state of being "in love" can awaken parts of us that have been lying most peacefully dormant – and that's a voyage of discovery![C]

Throughout her life, Madeleine wrote songs. Her husband feels that she concentrated on song-writing because, as a woman in the midst of family life (which Madeleine defined as 'the supermarket and the sink' – the petty necessities of domesticity irked her), the long periods of time needed for composing extended works rarely came her way.

She produced more than 60 'serious' songs (her adjective), and a substantial amount of material for the intimate revues with which she was involved in the 1950s. It was the sad fate of most revue music that, once a show had finished its run, nothing was ever used again, and its programme of highly entertaining items was unceremoniously discarded and forgotten. This is a great pity because, as Courtney Kenny observes, some revue songs are simply too good to be allowed to disappear, and one glance at the manuscripts of Madeleine's settings of some superbly funny lyrics makes you wonder why these are still in pencil, unpublished, unknown. He supplied me with *High in the Pines* (from *Child's Play*), the opening of which you can see on p.111. The songs belong, obviously, to the decade in which they were conceived, but their datedness only adds to their considerable charm. As a group they demonstrate Madeleine's expertise in sending up the popular musical styles of her day. Mischievous waltzes are her speciality, as in her wickedly witty entreaty to an indifferent pianist *not* to woo her with yet another performance when there were far better things to do (***Don't play your sonata tonight, Mister Humphries***). Her heartfelt lyrics to *Torch Song*, a blues (pp 50-51), will touch a chord with all women who try in vain to juggle family demands and a career. And a snazzy little number (*Spring and cauli*), penned specially for a Royal College of

Music 'do', perfectly displays her flair for writing impish pastiche: a rumba, shot through with topical musical quotations and sly references to her tutors and colleagues, this must have raised quite a smile when it was performed. At Micropress we have rescued and published quite a number of her 'show'songs, and the very brave people who have since tried them out (sometimes in drag) tell us that they are 'a hoot', and cause much merriment.

It is even more difficult to understand why only a few of Madeleine's serious songs were published in her lifetime (notably the *Three Shakespeare Songs*, 1949) and why, after her death, Roger initially had to work so hard to convince others of their worth. A 'cosy ballad', *Thankyou, Lord* (1953) was printed by Keith, Prowse and Co, but I understand it was severely 'messed about with' by the publisher, who removed many Dring-isms, presumably in a misguided bid to broaden sales. This is unforgivable behaviour. It is cause for great rejoicing that Thames Publishing printed five volumes of her songs (completely unmolested) in the 1990s and now, at last, her best material is accessible to more than the previously lucky few who held manuscript copies.

In spite of the sage advice from her teacher, Leslie Fly, cautioning her that 'You should always write your name and the date on your manuscripts because if you don't, anyone can pinch it',[D] Madeleine left the greater part of her work unmarked in this respect. She had a different perspective on Time from most of us and, perhaps because of this, she felt she had no need to fix a composition at a specific point in history; indeed, she often described music as 'timeless' and 'ageless'. She was more likely to put her current address on a manuscript than its date of completion. Alistair Fisher has spent much time and trouble in trying to date some of her songs, and his conclusions are documented in his dissertation of 2000 (University of Hull). Madeleine also hated editing her music ('it is a job I shirk!' she told Hemmer) and, consequently, we are confronted with a collection of largely anonymous, dateless, expression-mark-less pieces and, in spite of people's best efforts and considerable ingenuity, little prospect of ever being able to arrange them into chronological order! But if dates didn't matter to Madeleine, I really don't see why they should matter to us. (By the way, Mr Fly would be relieved to learn that nothing, thankfully, ever did get 'pinched'.)

Madeleine was a gifted singer and pianist, and so it was natural that she should be attracted to a genre which was useful to her as a performer. She was still taking singing lessons in her fifties, reporting that she felt both exhilerated and emotionally drained by the artistic effort required in the presentation of a song. Most of her soprano songs were written with herself in mind, and their high notes and wide range give an indication of her considerable vocal agility. At informal concerts she accompanied herself on the piano, as does Courtney Kenny – no mean feat – but she preferred to have an accompanist for anything public, although she did not work with any one pianist on a regular basis. Sometimes she played for singers when they performed her songs, but in her lifetime nobody except Madeleine herself consistently used her songs in their recitals. The songs bear no dedications to other people and were written, we must conclude, purely to suit herself.

With this thought in mind, the type of verse she chose to set will undoubtedly tell us a great deal about her personality. Given unlimited choice, which words did she select? The overriding theme, central to more than 40 of her songs, is Love, love in all of its guises, bringer of pleasure and pain. The protagonists in Madeleine's musical mini-dramas are frequently love-sick (*A poor soul sat sighing*; *Love is a sickness*; *Why so pale and wan, fond lover*) or smitten with unrequited love (*Come away, death*; *Who killed the clock*). In some songs, potential relationships are tentatively or audaciously encouraged (*Come away, come sweet love*; *Live, live with me*); in others, lovers angrily bewail lost romances and fickle partners (*The Cuckoo*; *The Faithless Lover*). Reconciliation is sometimes attempted (*Come let us now resolve*) but more usually the singer mocks the so-called delights of love, deplores its ephemeral nature and sometimes gives up the struggle altogether, with a wry smile and a shrug. A few songs – a very few – celebrate the satisfaction of a mutual love that endures.

Love is a universal theme, ripe for exploration and exploitation by all composers. However, while other songwriters investigated a wealth of alternative topics (travel, the sea, war, loss, magic, spirituality, the natural world, to name but an obvious few) Madeleine seemed unable to distance herself from her examination of love's potential for delight and despair, and returned to it time and time again, spinning it round to find ever-new angles of view. Three of her four song-sets deal exclusively with love. Only the Betjeman set is slightly more detached, although even here the *Nightclub Proprietress* wistfully recalls her lost loves, and *Business Girls* bathe sadly alone and unloved.

Did Madeleine feel she was unloved? We know that she was lonely, both in a physical sense, due to Roger's frequent absence for his orchestral work, and on a psychological plane, since she recognised few kindred spirits. She seems to have had difficulty in finding people to get close to, and spent much time by herself. It could be argued that her songs were a vehicle through which she could express her sense of isolation and apartness, and her perpetually unfulfilled desire to 'belong'. This is not to say, however, that her vocal output is one long outpouring of grief. Far from it. If it is true that her motivation in setting a certain type of text was to express, and thereby attempt to assuage, her inner pain, then through the process of composition she managed to transform this pain into something quite beautiful.

She drew on a wide variety of verse including Shakespeare, Herrick, Marlowe, Lear, Rossetti, Blake and Betjeman, and employed a multitude of musical styles, borrowing a huge and attractive array of compositional devices from many historical periods. Towards the end of her life she seemed to be settling down into a style which is an expert blend of American and French influences, but her last pieces indicate that she was ready to move on yet again in a more serious vein.

Madeleine's pot-pourri approach to composition is both irresistible and infuriating. Impossible to pigeon-hole, she constantly side-steps musical categorisation. In her songs, people have heard snippets of Sondheim, bits of Brubeck, fleeting moments of Barber and Poulenc; the composer Geoffrey Bush particularly enjoyed those songs which, in his opinion, had a 'touch of the Gershwins' about them; but there is also Strauss and Chopin, Dowland and Byrd, and even some mediaeval organum. The only element she lacks is the atonality of 12-tone serialism, a style she found aurally incoherent. Many of the songs have an intriguing old-new ambivalence about them, since they are inspired by archaic dance-forms, but brought up-to-date by complex, modern harmonies.

She was particularly drawn to the dance-rhythms of 16th century galliards and jigs, and frequently chose a compound metre where she could make full use of a favourite lilting rhythm: the rhythm of her name. Past ages are also invoked by the recurrent use of parallel harmonies where 4ths and 5ths, major and minor chords and even whole towers of notes are shifted en bloc for many phrases, giving the music a ringing resonance. Harpsichord figurations feature in her often intricate piano-writing; vocal lines sport decorative quaver and semiquaver runs, and ornamentation typical of bygone eras. But at the same time she was seduced by the warmth of contemporary popular harmonies, and revelled in the sounds of chords built from piled-up 3rds.

Three Shakespeare Songs, the first, and only, song-set that was published in her lifetime, is a fine example of Madeleine's ability instantly to set a mood by imaginative choice of musical material. *Under the greenwood tree* is a playful interpretation of Shakespeare's words, their sunny nonchalance being captured in a wayward, wind-blown accompaniment which tumbles and turns like a court jester, never settled, never still. The vocal line, as is usual with Madeleine, is dictated by the harmony (rather than generating it) and in consequence is angular, agreeably spiky, and full of arpeggios, more of an instrumental line than a vocal melody. Because she worked from a harmonic basis, she rarely wrote 'tunes'. Singers say that her lines are mightily difficult to pitch in the first instance, but the compensation is that they are impossible to forget once learned! An exception which proves the rule is the second of the Shakespeare songs, *Come away, death*, whose sultry melody is perfect for crooning. The well-rounded harmonies bring to mind the incomparable setting of *King David* by her one-time tutor, Herbert Howells. Verse 2 of the Dring is subtly extended to incorporate misty triplets which carry the sibilant alliteration of the 'thousand, thousand sighs to save'; sleepy enharmonic changes lull and caress the forsaken lover who slowly sinks, with the bass line, into a numbness of grief. Surely one of her very best compositions, if Madeleine had written no other music, *Come away, death* would suffice as eloquent testimony to her expressive power. In *Blow, blow thou winter wind* the energy returns, but the carefree enthusiasm of the opening song is replaced by a blacker humour, conveyed through stinging chromatic harmonies and arpeggio flurries which depict the harshness of the weather. This setting abounds with the sequential passages that Madeleine so frequently uses, and which give her music an appealing air of organised chaos: which key are we going to now? where will this phrase end up? whatever next? Who knows! She always leaves her musical options wide open, ever ready to take an unexpected turn and startle, tease or shock.

Madeleine turned her wit and charm on several other Shakespeare texts. In *Crabbed Age and Youth* she nimbly tailors the music to the words, colouring the chords to underline the contrast between juvenile vigour and crumbling old age. There is a delicious musical depiction of a gammy leg (b. 19 - 20). The flattened 7th in the melody gives it a jazzy feel, and the harmony fluctuates at will between major and minor, a favourite technique of Madeleine's. The final biting chord contains both a major and minor 3rd, and exactly this chord opens another song, *The Cuckoo*, where the flattened blue-note 3rd serves as a mocking variant on the bird's call. Here the main melodic line is a cascade of semiquavers which are taken up by the piano in verse 2 in an elegant counterpoint with the voice. This piano-voice interplay is rare in Madeleine's songs. Usually she gives the voice prominence, and the accompaniment, though invariably supplied with a wealth of interesting material, is only independent in the introductions, verse-links and codas. Occasionally it will boldly interrupt the voice with comments of its own, but this is generally reserved for comic effect. The typical Dring voice-piano relationship is clearly seen in *It was a lover*, a lively, rustic jaunt, effortless on the ear, very tricky to perform. The piano opens with a small, scalic figure which becomes the voice's key phrase. The cheeky piano introduction recurs as a verse-link and bursts into the coda, but otherwise the accompaniment consists of light chordal support and rhythmic interest, leaving the voice free to deliver the goods unhindered. Structurally *It was a lover* is as finely wrought as any art song, but its popular harmonies place it in the realm of the show-song; similar observations can be made about *Encouragements to a Lover* which, with its oom-pah accompaniment and vocal patter, would be very much at home in intimate revue.

Madeleine was bold enough to make her own versions of already frequently-set words, and for an appreciation of her setting of Shakespeare's *Take, O take those lips away*, here are the thoughts of John Amis:

> It is an Elizabethan poem couched in the musical language of today, exquisitely beautiful and passionate, as good a setting of the famous words as any I know, better I think even than the Warlock and as touching as the Quilter ... Dring has the same respect as Warlock for ... poems and the same insight into their heart.

Amis rates Madeleine very highly as a composer, as does tenor Robert Tear, who has called her 'One of the best, unknown, unrecognised English song-writers'. Her skill lies in her versatility and richness of musical invention. Take, for example, three songs which are unmistakably hers but are diametrically opposed to each other in content. *Come away, come sweet love* is, in essence, a Renaissance dance, but harmonically it is one of her most complex compositions. The main motif is a rising, sequentially treated figure above a pedal bass – a favourite technique of hers. The chordal writing is sumptuous, spicy and unpredictable; as Roger once said, while struggling to decode a complicated passage in an unpublished instrumental piece: 'You're never quite sure with Madeleine' – did she *really* intend that combination of notes? – for she rarely does the expected, or logical, thing; but on closer inspection it is clear that what she has written is right. Against this elaborately constructed song we can place the restrained simplicity of *Weep you no more, sad fountains*, where a melody which could have come straight from the pen of a master lutenist like Dowland threads its plaintive way between sprays of glittering droplets in the diamond-bright accompaniment. Different again is *The Faithless Lover*, an extraordinarily strong song, in all probability informed by personal experience. Menacing, and really quite vicious in parts, the song vividly evokes the anger and troubled spirit of an abandoned suitor. The music is percussive, changes metre incessantly and the words are spat out in irregular phrases; there is little room in which to catch breath and this increases the sense of tension.

Favourite Songs

Madeleine felt that her very best music was contained in her collections of settings of poems by Herrick and Betjeman. It seems, therefore, almost unkind to say that, to my ears, the opening song of the Herrick *Dedications* is less successful than most; but in *To Daffodils*, the harmonies outlined by the triplet broken chords of the accompaniment are not always convincing, nor are the written-in ritenuti at phrase-endings. Here, as in *Mélisande* (based on a French air), Madeleine deliberately simplified her style, and as I see it, the result is a bland, too-nice setting that is pleasant, but far from special. (Roger thinks differently! and perhaps so do you). On the other hand, *To the Virgins* is excitingly rhythmic and direct, and its tabor-inspired accompaniment drives a satisfyingly sturdy vocal line which requires very careful pitching. The hammered chords which propel this song foreshadow the very percussive piano style she later developed, and the central section illustrates the manner in which she often injected sudden changes of metre – a waltz into a march, a 5/8 section into a 6/8 piece – to enliven the proceedings (and trip up the dancers). The middle song, *To the Willow Tree*, is odd, but compelling. Its 5/8 metre gives it a little limp which emphasises the distress outlined by the words, and the strangely shaped, repeating melody wanders sadly through clanging piano chords. *To Music*, like *Come away, death*, opens with voice alone, and is an appeal for release from the suffering caused by love. Its measured tread and resounding, parallel chords create a feeling of solidity and great purpose, and Madeleine makes full use of her favourite flattened 7th, which lends the song a modal flavour. The final *Dedication, To Phyllis*, is a magnificently effective and taxing setting, very long by Madeleine's standards, more a playlet than a song. Herrick's vigorous verbal descriptions of a never-ending stream of gifts promised to his lady-love are matched by a highly inventive accompaniment and resourceful vocal line. It is interesting to consider two recordings of *To Phyllis*, one privately made at a concert, the other from a commercial c.d.(*The Far Away Princess*), both sung by Robert Tear. In the concert performance Tear's diction, phrasing, and vocal technique are faultless and his tone, as ever, is beautiful, but for some reason it all feels *too* perfect, gets boring and seems to go on forever! On the c.d., however, (a later recording) Tear has carefully rethought his interpretation, and here he 'messes about a bit', struts and swaggers, coos and cajoles, plays around with the words – and this time the listener is captivated. In the same way, all of Madeleine's songs respond if they are slightly 'over-performed'. Some require a flirtatious and irreverent approach, others demand a passionate intensity that would be destroyed by any attempt at humour, others are cool and serene, but all of them call for dramatisation and a determination to put over their essence at the expense (if need be) of what you might call a technically 'proper' rendition. In short, they don't work if they are done 'straight'. 'It is a terrible thing to be TEPID', said Madeleine at a CSPS talk in 1976, and there was nothing remotely luke-warm about her approach to life. She loved theatricality and performance of any kind, and engaged emotionally with everything she did. So must anyone who tackles her work.

    The song-set *Love and Time* is a journey through emotion: the listener is led by the hand through passion, and ensuing pain, to a hard-won peace. The settings are so effective, and speak so directly to the heart, that they must surely be a reflection of Madeleine's personal experience encapsulated in song. *Love and Time* is the only set of hers in which there is a musical link between the separate items. This connecting feature is a tranquil piano prelude whose theme is derived from a phrase in the second song. In *Sister, awake* the piano begins with a series of hollow, parallel chords embellished with grace notes. The accompaniment continues in a most delicate and delightful manner, full of air and light, stealing and then decorating the vocal melody which is also fresh and unusual, characterised by a raised 4th. Its blend of short, breathless phrases and high, arching lines perfectly convey the girlish excitement generated by the dawning of a new morn which, in this poem, is a metaphor for the awakening of love. In *Ah, how sweet it is to love!* Dryden's words are set with considerable rhythmic flexibility above a reassuringly steady accompaniment. The outer sections, framed by a short recitative, content themselves with only two melodic phrases, but the central part is capricious and mobile, led by a fluid and handsome melody which, as usual, is a law unto itself. At the start of the middle section, there is a very special moment. One bar is singled out; and through a sudden speed change and a pause, Madeleine says to us, **Listen**:

Love and Time with reverence use

It's a vitally important message, because how many of us do? – and surely we should. This song has a very American flavour, with its 4th-based melodies and chords of the 9th. *I feed a flame* is much more French. The gentle drum-tap of *Ah how sweet* becomes a perpetual quaver hammering, and clusters of unpleasant chords pound away above a bad-tempered bass, giving the impression of a persistent headache, a superlative portrait of pent-up emotion about to explode. After this onslaught the serene piano prelude returns, reharmonised in a slightly surreal way. These impenetrable clouds of bitonal sound slowly clear and Madeleine's 'brown' (i.e. warm, comfortable, safe) key of F major emerges. The *Reconcilement*, the concluding song of *Love and Time,* is a remarkable and unforgettable piece of writing, a long and wondrous vocal improvisation anchored by a pedal F. The soaring melismas are often in the shape of a great arch with a small dip at each end, like an expansive and generous physical gesture. The recurrent flattened 7th is spotlighted in the mysterious and magical coda, centred around the word 'quiet', and a final whole-tone vocal flourish, set against softly ringing parallel chords, provides an inspired ending to an outstanding song whose air of calm simplicity conceals the sophistication of its construction. Wanda Brister concludes that. 'based on Dring's beliefs in spiritualism and world harmony, combined with her gentle nature, *The Reconcilement* could have been Dring's personal anthem'. I definitely agree.

Two songs which speak the same musical language as those in *Love and Time* are *Love is a sickness*, which contains many essential Dring ingredients such as dance-rhythms, sequences and a madrigal-style refrain, and *Since there's no help, let us kiss and part*, another example of those Poulenc-influenced, chugging harmonies against whose fistfuls of competing notes the singer must pitch the melody with care. A gracefully arching phrase from *Sister, awake* is conspicuously used in the draft of an oboe piece (undated), suggesting that all these pieces are contemporary, generated from one common musical seed, planted very probably during Madeleine's trips to the USA.

The songs in the Betjeman set of 1976 are completely different. Sir John Betjeman, knighted in 1969, was named Poet Laureate in 1972. Dring selected 5 poems from an anthology of his which was published in 1970. *A Bay in Anglesey* is one of the most carefree songs that Madeleine wrote, a musical watercolour of a lazy sea, with the tide coming in. The vocal line takes a curious, winding path as if following the gentle exploration of the scene by the viewer's relaxed gaze. The dreamy accompaniment weaves a liquid line of quavers, tracing every lap and swoosh of the tide. *Song of a Nightclub Proprietress*, on the other hand, depicts a care-worn, disillusioned socialite for whom the sun has definitely set. In Madeleine's 'blue' key of G minor it is indeed a blues, sharply drawn but freely written, offering ample opportunity for the singer to develop the role in whichever direction is most appealing. The superbly slick and sleazy piano part brings to mind the *Mazurka* piano solo, and *Blue Air* from the *Colour Suite*. The third Betjeman song, *Business Girls*, is worlds apart from the seedy murk of the nightclub; the music is precise and clipped, and the words are almost entirely syllabically set. Particularly enchanting are the musical swirls of autumn wind in the piano verse-link and coda. *Undenominational* is a puzzling choice for the fourth item in the group; the words are delivered in the manner of a fierce hymn with an insistent dotted rhythm, and it does not fit comfortably with its companions. The final song, *Upper Lambourne*, is unconventional and demanding. Visually straightforward, this music has been the undoing of many a singer who took the challenge of the athletic vocal line and clanging consonants too lightly. Taxing, too, is the chordal piano part, which needs to be light and supple, and requires stamina to play it softly. The words speak of horses, but Madeleine rejects the obvious galloping-rhythms afforded by 6/8 and opts for a quirky 5/8. As ever, some of her most beautiful musical moments occur when she lets the piano loose; many of her lyrical verse-links could be developed into attractive pieces in their own right.

The original pencil versions of the Betjeman songs demonstrate how easily Madeleine wrote a piece once it had formed in her mind. Corrections to the script are very few – a chord is lightened here, a rhythm tightened up, an arpeggio reshaped – but there is little structural alteration, and rarely any remoulding of the melody. She kept no musical notebooks, but many of her manuscripts are dotted with 'trial runs'; most often these consist of several bars of ingenious chord-progressions, indicating that she thought harmonically, and not from a melodic or contrapuntal standpoint.

This approach is evident in the *Four Night Songs*, which are the last pieces that Madeleine wrote before she died suddenly in March 1977. One of them, *Separation*, she left unfinished, and the song was later completed by Roger. Madeleine had met poet and artist Michael Armstrong through her work for the Centre for Spiritual and Psychological Studies. The only time she ever ventured out of Britain alone was to visit Michael in the Canary Islands, just months before her death. Her settings of his verse are contemplative, mystic and intense, without the tiniest hint of the frivolity that chuckles through much of her other work. Inspired by Armstrong's painterly eye for natural detail, Madeleine finds powerful musical parallels for his strong visual imagery – moon and sun, night and stars, clouds, sparks and ice – as in the sharp staccato 'pebbles' in the introduction and coda to *Frosty Night*, and the streaming of the wind in *Holding the Night*. These poems speak of things that are hidden, forgotten and secret, and Madeleine responds with an introspective musical style. The widely arching vocal phrases we met in *Love and Time* are especially prominent in *Holding the Night*. The wandering, lonely harmonies in this song are held in check by long bass pedal notes, and the vocal range is characteristically broad: the melodic line covers a full two octaves. The same drifting-chords-over-pedal effect is found in *Through the Centuries*, whose haunting introduction begins with parallel major chords; these and the other main elements of the song – an eerie scale and a peaceful melody whose flattened 6th tugs at the heart – are cleverly woven into the coda, which also whispers the rhythm of 'centuries'. This is yet another example of Madeleine's gift for writing music which is exceptionally 'easy on the ear' and popular in feel, but totally serious in intent. Interestingly, the lyrics of *Through the Centuries* speak of reincarnation, and the reunion of soul-mates who find one another again and again over vast periods of time. Without doubt she believed in this. Her choice of poem could be interpreted as a reassurance to those she was about to leave behind, that they would be together again in a future life. Here are the words to Madeleine's final song, *Separation*:

> Out in the dark night
> the birds are asleep
> and you too are sleeping
> out of my reach
> held only in my thoughts.
>
> Of all the things in the world
> I love you most
> but I cannot get near you
> and you remain unknown.
>
> My love is waiting here for you
> to pick up and wear
> like a warm garment.
>
> At least enclose yourself
> within its folds,
> if only to keep out the cold.

I think you will agree that it is strange that this should be the last piece of music she wrote – almost as if she knew what was going to happen. The final text she set was 'Of all things in the world, I love you most. But I cannot...' Her husband Roger was left to complete the setting himself. Stranger still, the words of the poem echo the major theme of her life: they are an almost too-painful reminder of her perpetual struggle to reach out to others, only a few of whom ever stopped to listen.

The fragment of music that Madeleine left is deeply felt, combining hope, sadness and a quiet acceptance. The extended second beat of the pervading rhythm holds back the flow of the music with its recurrent hesitation; it is like the wary footfall of one who has resolved to move on, but is uncertain of what is to come.

Michael Armstrong, upon hearing of her death, wrote the following beautiful poem.

FOR MADELEINE

It is six months ago since you and I
Watched the house-high surf beyond El Golfo
And felt its shock of impact shudder beneath our feet,
As smoking waves smashed through subterranean caves
And raised swift screens of rainbows
Between us and the sinking sun.

Their violent rhythm hammered us
Until we shared a strange volcanic world –
A secret heaving birth of blue and white and black
That welded us within a new perception.

Now you are dead and yet not dead.
Eternity still hangs above a cup of rainbows
As fresh waves shake the cauldron
And the sun persists in setting in the west.
We still stand where we stood between the village and the sea,
Caught between the unreal and the real.

Madeleine Dring died abruptly, aged 53, on March 26 1977, in Streatham; the death certificate simply states 'brain aneurysm'. She collapsed while Roger was away from home, playing in an orchestra. She was buried in Streatham Cemetery, and the grave was reserved for 25 years. At the time of writing, Roger does not know if it is still there, and on my visit in 2009 I found nothing useful. Please contact me if you have information.

There is an intriguing bit of scribble inside the back cover of one of Madeleine's early notebooks. Here she is playing around with the number 7, noting that 7 seems to be of significance to her in very many ways. She observes that she was born on 7 September; she lived (at the time of the scribbling) at 7 Woodfield Avenue, Streatham; and, using techniques from numerology, she discovers that 'Dring = 7'. Later on, her address became 52 (5 + 2) Becmead Avenue in SW 16 (1 + 6), and so on in many other examples – this 'lucky' number seems to insinuate itself into all the corners of her life.

Was it just coincidence, then, that she died in 1977?

Final thoughts

How do you even begin to sum up a life like this one? The more I find out, the more astonished I am at how much she managed to achieve: as Howells bemusedly pondered, so do I – how, when and where did Madeleine do all that *work*?! She seems to have possessed an inexhaustible flow of imagination and energy, and she applied herself to her craft with amazing dedication. Had she lived longer, I have no doubt that she would have continued to have found texts that inspired her, and occasions to shake, and shock, the world with her antics.

It would be a daunting task to attempt to trace the development of her compositional style throughout four decades of musical activity. What strikes me most of all is how strong her music became, and how much she matured. By the 1970s all flippancy has vanished, and her work is direct, 'in-your-face', as they say, no holds barred. Roger is particularly taken with her *Toccata* (1976) which excites him with its rhythmic drive and urgency. A colleague of mine remarked that it sounds like 'a cross between William Matthias and Alberto Ginastera', and so it does; it is oceans away from the cosiness of 1950s revue. Whatever next?! This is what I continually ask, as each new piece is unearthed. There is still a pile of her early manuscripts awaiting attention, and much music out there, somewhere, that will probably never be found.

I don't think she was writing with an eye to posterity – she was composing simply because she needed to, and for her own contentment and satisfaction. But I hope she would be pleased to know that, 30 years later, musicians are still battling away to learn, and perform, her challenging pieces, and her name, and her work, lives on.

La Belle Coquine. This bird is of *French* origin and makes great play with its tail. During the mating season it will board the stalk of a hardy Daisy, swing to and fro and emit the cry 'Au secours'!

Very Interesting Appendix

Here follow some brief extracts from Madeleine's teenage diaries (age 13-18, 1936-45). I transcribed these for Roger, and made ink copies of the pencil drawings they contain. She wrote freely and candidly about her experiences, musical and otherwise. Her spelling is, on the whole, very individual! I have retained the original letterings and punctuation. I love her gossipy, conversational style, and most of the time I couldn't see what I was doing for laughing. I hope you find them enjoyable, too.

Here she is:

Madeleine Dring
7 Woodfield Avenue
Streatham S.W 16

Preface (if you bother to read it)
I am writing this — because I think it will be nice to look back on.
Thank you

[At home, and out and about]

Another dull day. We've got a new wireless set, 5 valve hope I've spelt it right. You can get many stations on it, further on in the book I shall write them down. I must learn how to work it you know.
….
I've got five bob and am crackers to learn Chopins Fantasia Impromtu in C sharp minor; I wrote to Miss Bull [teacher at the RCM] and asked her if I could be taught it at Col but she said I would get no ofical lessens on it but I could muck about with it if I liked; it wouldn't do me any harm She said she once tried to do Beethovens --- but it was a great pain to the whole house-hold; however it taught her how difficult it was.

[sketch: ME / as I am today with my color]

I had five bob on me on the 21st so mummy said if I could pick it up by hearing a gramophone record I could by one. So she went out and ordered me one…I really could have done it if it had not been for that syncopated bit, & mum thought hearing it on a record (you can alter the pace of the gramophone to quick or slow) I might be able to pick it up So it came, we put it on but the chap who was playing it did not play the base loudly enough for one to pick it up very quickly. We played it (record) several times & then put it away, and today I thought I'd have a shot at it; & I've got it

Gee! Wiz! Golly!
THE CRYSTAL PALACE HAS CAUGHT ALIGHT
(and I am afraid there is no hope of saving it)

I went out into the kitchen to clean my teeth (with much protest) about 8.10p.m. I looked out of the window & saw the sky was all red Phew! It gave me such a shock. I rushed out into the hall & cried "Mummy, can you see a red light in the sky?"…When Daddy & Cecil came in Dads first words were "The Crystal Palace's caught alight". Then we knew. It was also given out on the wireless on the 9 o.c. news. People are rushing up to see it & police are trying to keep them back. I know a girl that lives at the top of Streatham Common. Won't she have a 'glowing' account of it?
P.S. Sparks have flown into Beckenham & I am afraid it cannot be saved. Thus ends one of Londons greatest show places. The place where many famous people have been. That beautiful organ. Lend me a handkerchief somebody.

[1936] Dec 4th
The King wants to marry a Mrs Simpson an American society woman, but she's been divorced twice & is not of royal blood.

Please do not think these torn out pages are love letters or anything drastic. They are simply plans of Daddys. [an architect]

Dec 30th
Play went splendidly.

Had a very nice Christmas. Have had an idle time. I feel as if I shall burst if I don't do something naughty so have tied Cecils pygamas into knots & have written 'Gertcha' on Daddys clean pillow case in this blue pencil.

Barney [Miss Barne] wants me to compose.. a piece for violin & piano to play to Hudge [Hugh Allen] next term for special talent; so am doing so.

….
Am listening to the Proms. The programme is modern – terribly modern. I listened to the first movement of a Prokofiev (I had to borrow the Radio Times to spell his name) piano Concerto. It was – well it gave me the creeps but boy! It was wonderful. Now I am not quite sure wether I am listening to Ballet Music by Kodaly or a Bax Symphony No 4 (Oh! please forgive my awful ignorance) I think it is the latter. The others say it is a terrible noise but I like – well I can't exactly say 'like' it is a funny word. I'll say it *draws* me. Its very exhilarating somehow. Its – life. Life of a terribly modern & fast moving passionate present. Oh dear! This probably looks very 'bats in the belfry' – that's what

comes of trying to explain what you mean when you can't. And to make it still more impressive & creepy it is a very silent oppressive night with hardly any air. I'm all breathless – wether it is the weather or the music I can't say. Its no use people trying to compare it with Mozart or Beethoven or Handel you can't – its another realm in music …I was right; it is the Bax Symphony No 4. "What a blinkin' row says Father.

Me   Mummy   Cecil + Dad

(good thing we sent our luggage on wasn't it?)

….
Mummy took me to the Drs this morning because I have been feeling awfully rotten lately. He said there was nothing the matter with me except a bit of anemia again (blinkin' nuisance isn't it?) He said I may do games & Gym at school as long as I go steady & he has given me the same old green pills (If you bite them you're sick – he said so & I know because I did one day (but I wasn't *quite* sick) to be taken only twice a day – it used to be three times. Mummy bought me some malt & codliver oil on our way home. For dinner I had liver & a lot of spinach & a cup of spinach water (which looks & tastes like green stagnant water) (that was for supper) & I also had some carrots & these pills so I've made a good start haven't I? They say fair people are rather subject to anemia & I am very fair (I only mean my skin & hair silly!) although my hair is much darker & could not actually be called very fair though sometimes ('speccially when its been washed – I do *not* use peroxide) it looks quite blondy Its just ordinary fair hair but its not right – by my stupid white skin (so the schooldoctor says) it (my hair) ought to be red. Swizzle! Isn't it? Oh gosh! There is someone playing Chopin's

polonaise in A flat on the wireless BOTHER! They've turned it off or very soft or something. *I wish I was not in bed*

….

Mummy left me to rummage round while she did a bit of shopping. I nearly lost the 2nd Rachmaninov concerto, for I had it renewed, and left it on one of the empty shelves beside the music part, with some others I'd got. I was furraging round for nothing in particular (I ended by taking some more Rachmaninov), when a young man came along and began to do likewise, until he caught sight of my Concerto. He picked it up and began to study it carefully. He took quite a long time about it and I was going to say he could have it, when at length he put it down. He looked around and then picked up the book I'd got about composers in America…However he put that down too, and, having found a music book that I wanted, I picked the whole lot up and departed. I shan't leave books I want on the side there again, because I have such a heavenly time, floundering through the Rachmaninov.

....
[At the RCM]

Went up for grading exam on Friday and had Miss Gasgell [Lilian Gaskell]. She is a very nice, sensible lady. I can't write what she said but she did say an awful lot of nice encouraging things, and said that with most of us, our pieces were far in advance with our technique but because of this, they were not to be kept back. Instead of saying 'Will you play the scale of B flat major' she'd say 'See if you can do B flat major, I always think its such a beast' and the whole thing was more like a lesson except that she didn't keep stopping me, She discussed what grade I should be in and settled that I should work for VII which is the Advanced, asked about my composition and said I must play at a concert next term (my piano teacher had just said the same, outside the door) and a lot more but she did not give the impression of flattering, she was much too genuine, so that why I felt awfully pleased I had slogged. Miss [Jewel] Evans other pupil went in also and she was awfully pleased with us – she said we 'played like gods!' Mummy had a talk with her afterwards and she said she had heard about my composition so if I wrote something for piano, got it approved of by Mr [Leslie] Fly (which is something) she said she would let me play it at a concert next term. So whoopee! (How vulgar!)

The following Wednesday I had my fiddle lessen with [Miss Betty] Barne. The Teusday before that I played 'Vagabond' to Mac. She also thought that I'm like John Ireland. She said "God's given you a divine gift", put 'composition' down in her book – underlined it, and gave me five on five. She said there ought to be a sort of Ex+ for composers but she didn't think it would be fair to give me more marks than the others.

The Beginning of a garden party.
A very serious man.
Back view of a family.
The commedienne
'Darling!' etc.

Mr Fly said "There's a lot I want to say to you. He spoke about the different branches of composition you could take up. He said its early days now but it's just as well to think about these things as I'll have to decide one day. You can either write piano pieces for the Accociated Board examinations (theres more to that than one would imagine) or go in for bigger orchestral works and symphonies. Of course it all depends on what I'll turn out like, he says writing for the Board is a surer thing and there's more money in it and it's difficult to get publishers to look at symphonies and things. One has to think of beastly money if one hasn't dependant means, and Mr Fly says as far as he can see, he thinks I'll turn out to be a writer of piano music like he is. Of course, he said, he writes all kinds of things as well but you do want something you can be sure of. But it is early days to know what I'll be yet.

….
My piano teacher called a young man in on my lessen to hear my piano piece. He had bushy wavy hair, wore glasses and had big spaces between his teeth. He looked at me as though I was something from a museum and asked questions like a doctor. When I'd played he said "I say that's jollai good – play it again!" I began to enjoy myself and played it again. "Where doo yoo get your style of harmonies from?" he asked. My piano teacher said "She doesn't know" I said "I haven't the faintest idea" Many times that answer has come in useful.

People I know

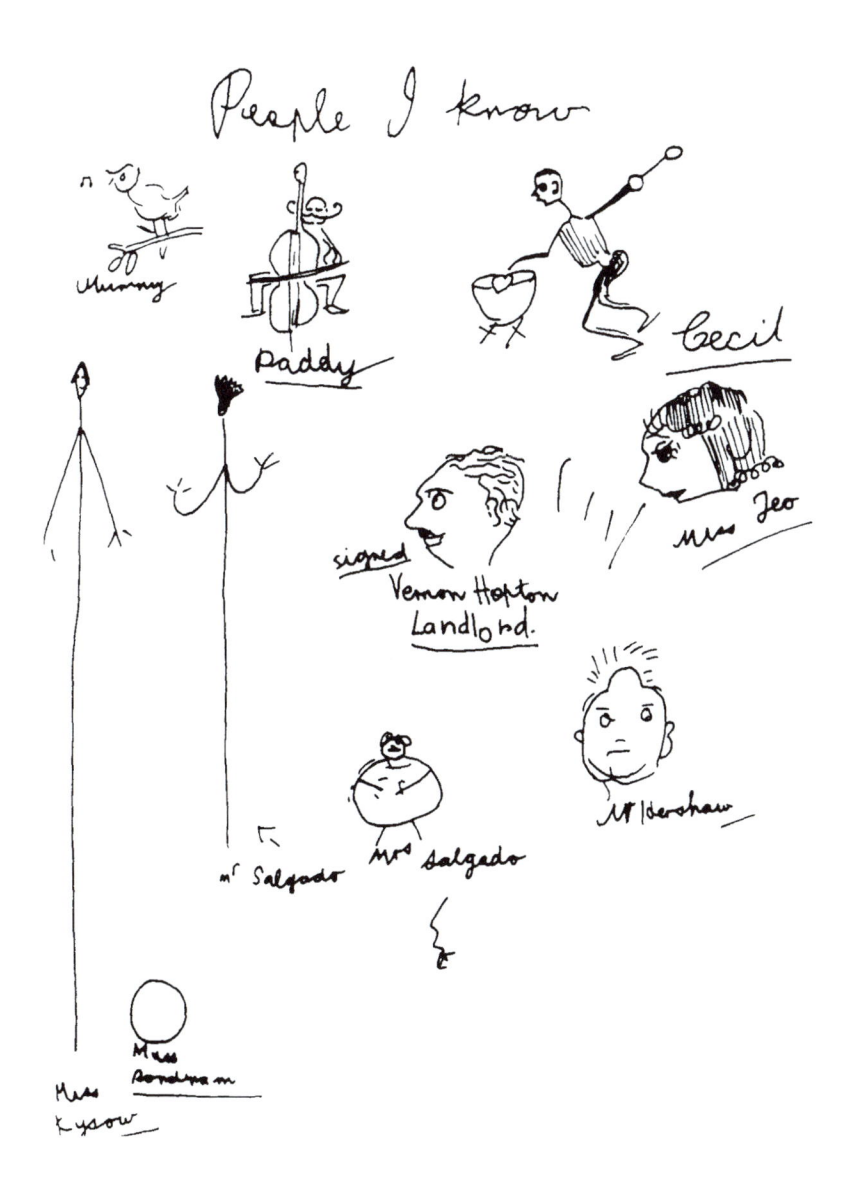

Mummy

Paddy

Cecil

signed Vernon Hopton Landlord.

Miss Jeo

Mr Salgado

Mrs Salgado

Mr Hershaw

Miss Boardman

Miss Kysow

On Friday I had another orchestral rehearsal. In the afternoon at school…we did A Tradgerdy Rehearsed by Sheridan. We pushed back the desks and acted it. I was Tilbarina, the heroine, and Graziella was Don Tirolo Whiskerandos, my lover. That play really is a scream! My part's great fun, especially as I have to see a vision.

We did the Bach concerto in orchestra. Parts were missing so Eugene & I went hunting for them, but we were unsuccessful. Some beastly seconds found them on their stands at last. We also did the Flute Suite. I felt terribly tired…Had learned previously that morning from Mr Fly, that Maurice [Browning] was also going to play my pieces at the Special Talent concert on Monday. This bowled me over completely. Maurice himself had not known it until the Saturday before…Here he was, going to play them in front of goodness knows whom on Monday and I hadn't once heard him play them. Of course he was a darned good pianist and under Miss Aspinall, but I wished I'd heard him play the things.

It was almost time for orchestra when we adjourned upstairs, but Mr Fly said he must look at my new piece. The theme is good and there's a lovely chord at the climax, and a very good piece of writing in the left hand, but it isn't quite 'me' yet. I'm to keep the theme and try again. He said I mustn't worry because I don't get it going first time. He looked at one or two ideas in my pad, and at the drawings (I do the most ridiculous caricatures over anything that's in rough) and said I mustn't rub out the drawings because he likes them.

In Hans old mill, his three black

    cats

Watch the bins for the thieving

    rats

Whisker & claw they crouch in

    the night

Their five eyes gleaming gold &

    bright

Squeaks from the flour sacks

squeaks from

    where the cold wind stirs on

the empty stair

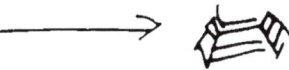

Squeaking & scampering every

    where

The other week I was waiting about for Miss Barne. She didn't come so I began to look along the different rooms for her. I looked in Herbert Howells room several times (partly for devilment) and every time I looked at him he seemed to be looking out at me... Besides, I was pretty thunderstruck by his pupil – a really remarkable specimen with ridiculously long hair and glasses.

So poor old H.H. must know me by now. Theres not another person in the College I've run into by fate so much. I can't say I dislike him though, in spite of the inconvenience he's caused us. I was reading a book about contemporary British composers by Joseph Holbrooke, the other week. It came out about thirteen years ago. It was rather interesting because many of the composers mentioned, who are leading lights today, were not nearly such big men then. I laughed when I read a chapter devoted to Herbert Howells. Holbrooke said of him 'it looks as though Herbert Howells almost has a style, if he is going to develop one' (or words to that effect), and he termed him a 'cheerful youth' Oh boy! How I'd love to thrust that under Herbies nose now! But the book certainly said some nice things about him. He got the best criticizm of all – better even than our mighty Vaughan Williams.

Night at the Opera

my dear! I couldn't touch a thing!
The chemist
This way sir!
a gracious lady
The young man with the sports car
A learned gentleman
'Well! I do think you might have told me about it!'
Mrs 'Igginson.
'Noo!' Ai nevah touch alchohol'

'Things shoved in my mouth'

Madeleine in the title role 'Unaida', with Anthony Newlands,
Players' Theatre production 1957.

Madeleine with son Jeremy at Daytona Beach, 1960s

Having fun!

On tour in Florida 1966

An early London portrait.
(eyelashes, eyebrows and lip bow have been inked in, presumably by Madeleine, to emphasise the film-star look!)

A late London portrait

Madeleine Dring.

KEY TO REFERENCES IN THE TEXT

C   Madeleine gave three talks for the *Centre for Spiritual and Psychological Studies* in London, contributing to larger events which included papers on the Visual Arts and Poetry: The Role of the Arts (6.12.1975); Living Creatively in the New Age (18.5.1976); Intimations and Expressions of Another Reality, in Life and Through Art (3.7.1976). Madeleine's hand-written lecture-notes are with RL.

D   Diaries. Between 1935-1943 Madeleine kept regular diaries, using a series of paperback exercise books. The exact dates of the entries are not always clear. Madeleine's colourful spellings have been retained. All of the diaries have been transcribed by Ro Hancock-Child, and the originals and transcription are with RL.

H   indicates that the information has been taken from typed copies of Madeleine's letters to the American composer Eugene Hemmer during the period 1967-1977. Extracts reproduced courtesy of Lance Bowling, Cambria Records.

MA   from Madeleine's letters to Michael Armstrong.

N   Notes. Madeleine made a considerable amount of notes for her CSPS talks (see C above), not all of which were used in the lectures themselves. At many other times in her life she jotted down quotations, prayers and other nuggets of wisdom which appealed to her. She recorded her dreams in note-form in order to analyse them; she often scribbled down ideas for lyrics and plots. She appears to have liked the luxury of a 'new book' to write in: on many occasions she used only the first few pages of a sketchbook or writing pad, and then abandoned it in favour of a fresh one. None of these notes are dated, but they provide a fascinating insight into her thought-processes and methods of working. All with RL.

RL   Roger Lord

ILLUSTRATIONS in the main text are taken from Madeleine's *Book of Birds*, a collection of very silly cartoons with hilarious captions.

Select BIBLIOGRAPHY

BANFIELD, Stephen, *Madeleine Dring*, in *New Grove Dictionary of Music and Musicians* vol.7 2nd ed. London Macmillan 2001

BRISTER, Wanda, *The Songs of Madeleine Dring: organising a posthumous legacy*, Doctoral document, University of Nevada, Las Vegas 2004

BRISTER, Wanda, *The Songs of Madeleine Dring*, Journal of Singing May 1 2008

British Composer Profiles, written & compiled by Gerald Leach, British Music Society publication

DAVIS, Richard, *Singer's Notes: 7 Shakespeare Songs of Madeleine Dring,* South Central Music Bulletin Vol 111 no 1 Fall 2004

DAVIS, Richard, *The published songs of Madeleine Dring,* Journal of Singing 63, no 4, Mar 2007

DRING, Madeleine, *Diaries 1935-1943*, typescript, transcribed by Ro Hancock-Child 1997

FISHER, Alistair, *The Songs of Madeleine Dring and the evolution of her compositional style* Bachelor's thesis University of Hull 2000

GOUGH MATTHEWS, Michael, *Madeleine Dring*, (obituary) in *RCM Magazine* Vol 73 Nos. 2-3, Oct 1977 p49.

LORD, Roger, *Madeleine Dring*, in *New Dictionary of National Biography* 2004

TWIGG, Victoria, *Madeleine Dring,* Thesis, Trinity College, London, 1982 (copy at GB-Lmic).

WHARTON, Sara, *Madeleine Dring (1923-1977), profile of a miniaturist* Dissertation for RCM 1977

In addition to this, there is a wealth of information about Madeleine available on the Internet, where you will find many small articles and commentaries on her life and work.

Please visit our website **www.madeleinedring.com** for links and more information.

Dring Discography – much expanded!

A mixture of vinyl/cassette/compact disc/on-line download

Many of these recordings are no longer commercially available (most of those from about 2000 onwards are) – but don't despair, because someone, somewhere, will have a copy for you to listen to, and if all fails please contact me, and I will find one for you.

Argo ZK 55
Harmonica Recital (Tommy Reilly/harmonica, James Moody/pno)
includes *Italian Dance*

Black Box CD BBM1084
London Conchord Ensemble (Daniel Pailthorpe/fl, Emily Pailthorpe/ob, Julian Milford/pno)
 includes *Trio for flute, oboe and piano*

Blue Griffin cat. 125 (2008)
Spectral Trio (Jan Eberle/ob, Kimberly Schmidt/pno)
includes *Danza Gaya* for oboe and piano

Boston Records BR1019CD (2001)
The Winning Program (Nancy Ambrose King/ob, Eric Dalheim/pno)
includes *Three Piece Suite*

Boston Records B0000477OK
Evocations (Nancy Ambrose King/ob) includes *Italian Dance*

Boston Records 1055 (2003)
Amy Porter and Nancy Ambrose King (Amy Porter/fl, Nancy Ambrose King/ob, Phillip Bush/pno)
includes *Trio for flute, oboe and piano*

Cala Records CACD0544 (2006)
Chamber music for flute (Jeanne Baxtresser/fl, Joseph Robinson/ob, Pedja Muzijevic/pno)
 includes *Trio for flute, oboe and piano*

Cala Records 518 (2008)
New York Legends: Joseph Robinson:oboe includes a Dring piece

Cambria C 1014 (1979)
Piano Music by Germaine Tailleferre and Madeleine Dring
(Leigh Kaplan, Susan Pitts)
includes *Colour Suite*; *Caribbean Dance*; *Valse Française*; *Danza Gaya*

Cambria C 1015 (1980)
Dring Dances! (Leigh Kaplan/pno, Louise di Tullio/fl, Robin Paterson/pno)
Three Dances; *Moto Perpetuo*; *Jig*; *March – for the New Year*; *Valse Française*; *Waltz Finale*; *WIB Waltz*; *Sarabande*; *Tango*; *Italian Dance*; *Tarantelle*

Cambria C 1018 (1988)
Romantic Sax – Echosphere (Paul Stewart/sax, Deon Price/pno)
includes *Three Piece Suite*

Cambria CT 1020
Songscape (Margery MacKay/vce, Leigh Kaplan/pno) includes *Five Betjeman Songs*; *Love Lyric (Who killed the clock)*; *Four Night Songs*; *Elegy (Good people all)*; *Encouragements to a Lover*

Cambria CD 1065 (1993)
Adventures in music-making with the Dale-Haddons, duo-pianists
includes *Lilliburlero*; *Tarantelle*

Cambria CD 1084 (1996)
Leigh Kaplan plays Madeleine Dring (Leigh Kaplan, pno, with Louise di Tullio/fl, Susan Pitts/pno, Robin Paterson/pno): *Colour Suite; Valse Francaise; Waltz Finale; American Dance; Jig; Caribbean Dance; Danza Gaya; Tarantelle; Italian Dance (2 pnos); 3 pieces for flute and piano: Wib waltz, Sarabande, Tango*

Cambria CAMCD-1125
Clariphonia (Berkeley Price/cl, Deon Nielsen Price/pno)
includes an arrangement of *3-piece suite*

Camerata 303338 (1997)
(William Bennett/fl, Clifford Benson/pno) includes *WIB Waltz*

Carlton Classics B0000245C4 (1998)
Nettle and Markham in England (David Nettle and
Richard Markham, 2 pianos)
 includes *Fantastic Variations on Lilliburlero no.1*

CC2016, Oboe Classics
Ambache chamber ensemble
includes *Trio for oboe, bassoon and keyboard*

Crystal CD727 (2004)
The Poetic Oboe (Andrea Gullickson/ob, Karen Emms/pno)
 includes *3-piece suite*

Dinmore Records DRD032
Love and Time (Michael Hancock-Child/baritone,
 Luise Horrocks/soprano, Ro Hancock-Child/pno):
3 Shakespeare Songs;The Cuckoo;The Enchantment;Crabbed Age and Youth; It was a lover and his lass;Take O take those lips away;Encouragements to a lover;5 Betjeman Songs; My Proper Bess; Come live with me; What I fancy I approve;Dedications;Love and Time (song-cycle);Through the Centuries;
 piano pieces: *Polka;Mazurka;Nightfall;Cuckoo Dance; Spring*

Dunhelm Records DRD0237
The Tend'rest Breast, setting of women's poetry
(Georgina Colwell/voice, Nigel Foster/pno)
includes *Don't play your sonata tonight, Mister Humphries*

Dutton Labs UK (2007)
British Music for Flute, Oboe and Piano
(John Anderson, Nancy Ruffer, Helen Crayford)
 includes *Trio for flute, oboe and piano*

Ensemble ENS 155
The Menagerie (Catherine Pierard, Susan Bickley, Julius Drake)
 includes duet *Pelicans*

Erase E0679
Let me see you Smile (Courtney Kenny/voice & pno)
includes *High in the Pines* (from *Child's Play*)

Erase LMSYS04
American Cabaret Songs from 1950-2000
(Courtney Kenny/voice & pno) includes *American Dance*

Helios 55159 (2004)
In praise of woman (Anthony Rolfe-Johnson/voice, Graham Johnson/pno) includes *Crabbed Age and Youth*; *To the Virgins*

Hyperion CDA 66289
(Sarah Walker/voice, Roger Vignoles/pno)
includes *Song of a Nightclub Proprietress*

Hyperion HYPE 66709 (1992/3)
In praise of Women (Anthony Rolfe-Johnson/tenor, Graham Johnson/pno) includes *Crabbed Age and Youth*; *To the Virgins*

Hyperion 67316 (2002)
Peacock Pie (Martin Roscoe/pno and Guildhall Strings)
includes *Festival Scherzo*

Hyperion HYP67457
London Pride (Catherine Bott/voice, David Owen Norris/pno)
includes *Business Girls*

HP7707
Daystream Dances:Women composers for oboe
(Cynthia Green Libby/ob, Peter Collins/pno)
includes *3-piece suite*

IBS 1024 (Canada)
Entre Nous (Musica Viva and Friends)
includes *Trio for Flute, Oboe and Piano*

Intriplicate int01 (2004)
(Claire Filhart/fl, Sally Richardson/ob, Claire Dunham/pno)
Includes *Trio for flute, oboe and piano*

Loud & Bunch Productions
If music be the food of love (Bruce, Colwell duo)
includes *The Cuckoo; Take o take those lips away;
It was a lover and his lass*

MSV 1838/ DAV1104(1995)
The Deutz Trio (Paul Edmund Davies/fl, Roy Carter/ob,
John Alley/pno) includes *Trio for Flute, Oboe and Piano*

Meridian MER KD89018 and CDE 84386 (1998)
The Far Away Princess (Robert Tear/tenor, Philip Ledger/pno):
Three Shakespeare Songs; *Mélisande*; *My Proper Bess*; *Dedications*;
Five Betjeman Songs; *Four Night Songs*

Micropress MPSCD2001 (2009) and Chandos download
Red Glory (Ro Hancock-Child/pno): *Polka; Spring; 4 Early Pieces:
Vagabond, Willows, Polka, Waltz with apologies; Country Dance arr.
RL; Nightfall; Mazurka, Pavane & Ländler; Spring Pastorale; Colour
Suite; Moto Perpetuo; Valse Française; Cuckoo Dance; Jubilate;
Times Change; Romance arr. Ro H-C; Prelude & Toccata 1976;
Caribbean Dance*

MRC classical A0284-CD (2000)
Madeleine Dring Collected Chamber Works (Margaret Lynn/pno, Jane
Finch/ob, Martin Cratt/bsn, with Joanne Boddington/fl): *Trio for flute,
oboe and piano; Polka for flute and piano; Colour Suite; Danza Gaya;
3-piece suite; Trio for oboe, bassoon and piano*

Oboe Classics label
Melodic Lines (Jeremy Polmear/ob, Diana Ambache/pno,
Philip Gibbon/bsn)
includes *Trio for oboe, bassoon and piano*

Pearl/Opal SHE CD9627
Shakespeare and Love (Gillian Humphreys/vce, Courtney Kenny/pno)
  includes *Come Away, Death*

Quartziade QTZ-006 (2007)
Quartz 11 (Quartz Ensemble: Thierry Cammaert/ob,
Christophe Postal/pno)
  includes *Idyll* for oboe and piano

Quartziade QTZ-007 (2007)
Tea Time (Quartz Ensemble: Gerard Noack/fl, Thierry Cammaert/ob,
Christophe Postal/pno)
  includes *Trio for flute, oboe and piano*

SRS/OG/2050
Songs of Madeleine Dring (Janet Johnston/sop, Ray Holder/pno)
  includes *Fantasy Sonata for piano solo*

Swinsty FEW124 (cassette)
(Jill Crowther/ob, David Baker/bsn, Alan Cuckston/pno)
  includes *Trio for oboe, bassoon and piano*

Toshiba/EMI TOCE 6850
Romance (Charlotte de Rothschild/sop, Julius Drake/pno)
  includes *The Cuckoo*

Unic DK PCD9121
(Jeremy Polmear, Diana Ambache/2 pianos) includes *Danza Gaya*

Unicorn Kanchana B00000E98L (1993)
Sweet Melancholy (Jeremy Polmear/ob, Diana Ambache/pno)
  includes *Danza Gaya* for oboe and piano

White Line cat. 250 (2001)
British Light Music Festival includes Danza Gaya

White Line cat. 510 (2004)
Halcyon Days: a Treasury of British Light Music (conductor Paul
Murphy, Raphaele Wind 6tet) includes *Danza Gaya*

(**archive, not 'professional' recordings**)

Madeleine Dring playing and singing her own compositions (variable sound quality but fascinating listening): *Snowman; I've been roaming; Jubilate; Spring Pastorale; Moto Perpetuo* (an extraordinary rendering!); *Caprice; Caribbean Dance* (with Ray Holder); c.d. with RL

Rose Hill sings *Deirdre* (from *Four to the Bar*); tape copy with RL

Betty Artis plays Dring piano music: includes *Mazurka, Pavane & Ländler; Valse Française; Moto Perpetuo*; c.d. with RL

Stop press....

People are still approaching me with tales of Madeleine's uncanny psychic abilities. Tony Halstead, very well-known horn player and at one time a fellow-performer with Roger Lord in the LSO, told me (July 2009) that he met Madeleine at a concert in the 1970s; she said to him 'You're a composer, aren't you?' to which he replied 'How do you know', and she said 'I just know'. She told him he ought to write something for the LSO, and he thought, never in a million years would it get played if I did – but he did write something, and a year later it did get played...

Catalogue of known Dring compositions

Key to abbreviations of publishers' names

A	Arcadia	ME	Mozart Edition
AB	Associated Board	N	Nova
C	Cambria	OUP	Oxford University Press
H	Heinrichson	P	Peters
I	Inter Art	T	Thames
L	Lengnick	W	Weinberger
M	Micropress Music		

Some useful addresses:

Cambria Music c/o Lance Bowling, Box 374, Lomita, CA 90717 USA

Alfred Lengnick & Co, 20 Fulham Broadway, London SW6 1AH

Micropress, The Blue House, 14 Brooksmead, Bognor Regis, West Sussex PO22 8AS

Oxford University Press, Great Clarendon Street, Oxford OX2 6DP

Peters Edition Ltd, 2 – 6 Baches Street, London N1 6DN

Thames Publishing, enquiries to 14 Barlby Road, London W10 6AR

Josef Weinberger c/o Sean Gray, 12/14 Mortimer Street, London W17 3JJ

Dates of composition are given, if known, and publication date follows in brackets, with identifying initial/s, see above. If no publication information is given, the work is either still in ms form (mostly with RL and Ro H-C) or its whereabouts is currently unknown.

Arrangements by Madeleine Dring (none published, mss with RL)

Brook, The (Dolores)
Cherry Ripe
Every Time we say Goodbye (Cole Porter)
Enchantress, The (Hatton/Chorley)
For you and me (Pinsuti)
First Love
Fan Song
I am so cosmopolitan   (Lehar)
In the still of the night (Cole Porter)
I often ask (Cole Porter)
If (Pinsuti)
I've been roaming (C E Horn)
I'd choose to be a daisy
Last Night
Love has eyes
Lover   (Rogers & Hart, incomplete)
Nina   (Pergolesi)
Nell Gwynn's Song (Raymond Roze)
Meeting of the Waters, The
Spider and the Fly, The (a duet)
Where, oh where (Cole Porter)
When we meet (Hope Temple)
Whenas I view your comely grace

Dramatic, unpublished

Cupboard Love
1-act satirical opera (D F Aitken) sop, bar, spoken part + pf

Duets / Part-songs

Bustopher Jones (T S Eliot)
    5 male vv + pf
Jim Jay
    2-pt unacc.
Pelicans (Edward Lear)
    Duet
Phyllida and Corydon
    Duet sop/bar
Pigtail, The (A von Chamisso)
    Duet (1963OUP)
Seagull of the Land-under-Waves (Skye Air)
    5 male vv
To sea, to sea, the calm is o'er
    Duet sop/mezzo (alto)

Incidental Music for Radio / TV / Theatre / Revue

20.12.1941
The Emperor and the Nightingale, adapted from Andersen by MD. Parry Opera Theatre, London (RCM), incidental music and production by MD.

1945
Apple Pie Order, costume comedy by T B Morris, incidental music by MD (2pf).

October 1946
Tobias and the Angel, play by James Bridie. Music composed, arranged and played by MD (Arts Council commission).

May 1947
Waiting for ITMA, ballet, BBC TV, produced by Royston Morley. Music by MD, *A song of the wind*, and incidental music.

26.5.1947
Somebody's Murdered Uncle, who-dun-it. Book & lyrics D F Aitken. BBC Radio Home Service, producer Tom Ronald.
Songs by MD including *I should have trusted you, darling*; *There's nothing to stop us now, dear*.

1948/9, 1950, 1955/6
The Wild Swans, children's play by Angela Bull. Rudolf Steiner Theatre, London, and RCM. Incidental music by MD, Lilian Harris and Freda Dinn.

1950
The Ghostly Legacy, play by Margaret Rubel. Incidental music by MD.

March 1951
The Fair Queen of (Yuch) Wu, 1-act opera, Chinese dance-drama. BBC TV, produced by Philip Bate, choreography Felicity Andreae (Gray). Book by D F Aitken.
Music for ob, cor ang, harp, str 4tet & solo singers MD.

1951, 1956/7
The Marsh King's Daughter, children's play by Angela Bull. Rudolf Steiner Theatre, London, and RCM. Incidental music by MD.

22.4.1953 (run)
Airs on a Shoestring, intimate revue directed by Laurier Lister. Royal Court Theatre, London. MD wrote words & music for *Sing high, sing low* and music for *The Model models* (2001M), *Snowman* (2001M), *Films on the cheap side at Cheapside*.

1953/4
The Scarlet Crab-Apple, play by Angela Bull. Rudolph Steiner Theatre, London, and RCM. Incidental music by MD.

December 1954 (run)
Pay the Piper, intimate revue directed by Laurier Lister.
Saville Theatre, London.
Intro music and one song by MD.

June 1955
From Here and There, intimate revue directed by Laurier Lister. Royal Court Theatre, London. MD wrote music for *Resolutions* and *Life Sentence*.

20.12.1955 – 7.1.1956 (run)
Fresh Airs, intimate revue directed by Laurier Lister. Theatre Royal, Brighton; Comedy Theatre, London. MD wrote words of *Witchery* and words & music for *Mother Knows* and *Miss Spenser*.

October 1958 (short run)
Child's Play, revue by Sean Rafferty directed by Reginald Woolley. Players' Theatre, London.
MD wrote music for *Overture, Case History, Daisy 1956, Soliloquy, Hearts and Arrows, Lullaby, High in the Pines* (2000M).

12.3.1959 (short run)
The Buskers by Kenneth Jupp, directed by Toby Robertson.
Arts Theatre Club, London.
Incidental music by MD.

November 1960
Little Laura, BBC TV film series (children's cartoon). Drawn by V H Drummond, directed by Oliver Postgate. MD wrote and played soundtrack. (this can be viewed on **tvrage.com**)

1961/2 (run)
Four to the Bar, intimate revue directed by Laurier Lister.
Criterion Theatre, London.
MD wrote music for Deirdre.

19.10.1961
The Jackpot Question by John Bowen, directed by
Toby Robertson, ATV. Music by MD.

24.7.1963
The Provok'd Wife, play by John Vanbrugh. Directed by Toby Robertson, Vaudeville Theatre, London. MD wrote music for
Oh lovely nymph; *When yielding first*; *Fly, fly you happy shepherds*; *What a pother of late*.

June 1964
The Lady and the Clerk, play by Julian Orde, ATV, produced by Royston Morley. Incidental music by MD.

1964
I can walk where I like, can't I?, ATV play. Incidental music by MD.

1965
When the wind blows, play by P Nichols, ATV, directed by
 Graham Evans. Incidental music by MD.

1966
Variation on a Theme by Terence Rattigan, ATV play.
Incidental music by MD. (2 pf)

21.3.1966
Ivanov, ATV play. MD wrote three arrangements for 'cello + piano, and one original piece *Sparrow, sparrow*.

1966 *Helen and Edward and Henry*, ATV play.
 Incidental music by MD.

19 - 24.7.1971
The Real Princess, ballet, directed by Mari Bicknell.
Theatre Royal, Bury St. Edmunds. MD wrote piano-duet score.
(Arts Council commission.)

?1930s/40s
Haymaking Party, mime by Margaret Rubel.
Royal College of Music, London. Incidental music by MD (2 pf).

?1961 *The Whisperers*, play by R Nicholson & Denis Webb, ATV. Incidental music by MD.
Up and Away, musical show, book & lyrics by C Mitchell. 29 musical items by MD, all lost.
A Spring of Love, ATV. Incidental music by MD.

Instrumental

Clarinet and Piano

Jack Brymer Clarinet series (1976 W)

Elementary Book 1: *Jog Trot*; *Evening Song*; *Rigadoon*; *Lazy Day*

Ensemble

Dance in C	pf+str
Minuet in F	2vln+vla+cell+bass
Tango	cell+str orch+pf. For Lance Bowen (Jan 1948)
Festival Scherzo	solo pf+str orch, 1951
Trio (fl+ob+pf)	Jan 1968 (1970W) for Musica da Camera
Trio (ob+bsn+hpd)	1971/2 (1986N) for Athenaeum Ensemble

Flute and Piano

Three pieces (1983C):   *WIB Waltz*; *Tango*; *Sarabande*

Harmonica and Piano

Harmonica Suite (1984N)

Treble Recorder

Six Pieces (easy) (L)

Oboe and Piano

Italian Dance	(1960A, W)
Polka	(1962A)
Waltz	(1983C)
Tango	(1983C)
Sarabande	(1983C)
Three-piece Suite (1984N) arr. RL from *Harmonica Suite*	
Danza Gaya	(ME)
Idyll	May 1948 (2001M) arr. RL from Viola *Idyll*

Viola and Piano

Idyll	May 1948 (2000M)

Violin and Piano

Piece in D 3/4
Piece in C
Piece in D 6/8
Sonata B min 1mmt
Reverie
Allegretto
'Boldly', B min
'Lightly', D

In Happy Mood	c.1937
Impromptu	c.1938
Romance	Feb.1939
Country Dance	(1981/2 AB)

Piano pieces (ms in existence) (solo unless otherwise stated)

Chinese Dance	(G flat maj)
Caprice	(G maj) ms incomplete but MD recorded it in full (anyone like to take down the notes?!)
Hooligans	
Pastorale	(G maj, incomplete)
Prelude	(A min, incomplete)

Romance (B maj)	
Valse Joyeuse (G maj) (? pub. Arcadia)	
Fantasy Sonata	c.1938 (1948L)
Vagabond	Feb 1939 (2000M)
Willows	May 1939 (2000 M)
(untitled) E maj	May 1940
Prelude (Cshp minor)	1942
Polka	1942 (2000M)
Waltz	1942 (2000M)
Prelude	1942
Jig	by 1947 (1948L) ded. Muriel Liddle
3 Fantastic Variations on Lilliburlero	(1948L) 2 pf
Prelude and Toccata	(1948L)
Tarantelle	(1948OUP) 2 pf
Festival Scherzo, *or*	1951 (1964ME)
Nights in the Gardens of Battersea (pf+str orch)	ded. Kathleen Cooper
Sonata	(1951L) 2pf
Five by Ten:	(1952L)

Book 1: *Skipping Song; Roundelay; Pecking Sparrows; Courtiers Dance*
Book 2: *The Horse Rider; Minuet*
Book 3: *Remembered Waltz; Sad Princess*
Book 4: *Nightfall*
Book 5: Spring

Jubilate	1953 (2002M)
March – for the New Year	(1954H, P) ded. Kathleen Cooper
Caribbean Dance (*Tempo Tobago*)	(1959I) also 2pf
The Soldiers Pass	1959
Spring Morning	(1959W)
Little Minuet	(1959W)
The Three Ducklings; Song of the Bells; Hornpipe	(1960W)
American Dance	(1960A, W)
Italian Dance	(1960A, W) also 2pf; ob+pf; orch
Waltz Finale	(1961A, W) also 2 pf
West Indian Dance	(1961A, W) also 2 pf
By the River	(1961R)
The Little Waggon	(1961R)
Three French Dances: *Rigaudon; Berceuse; Gigue*	(1962OUP)
Polka (also fl+pno;ob+pno)	(1962A,W)
Colour Suite (5 Rhythmic Studies for Piano)	(1963A)

Pink Minor; Red Glory; Yellow Hammers; Blue Air; Brown Study
Up and Away *(12 short pieces for teaching)* (1963OUP)

Four Piano Pieces: Stately Dance; Whirlwind;
Song without Words; Pastorale   (1964L)
Four Duets   (1964W) pf 4 hands
May Morning; Little Waltz; The Evening Star;
Morris Dance Danza Gaya (rhumba)
2pf, also ob+pf; ww ens+guit+bass   (1965ME)
Twelve pieces in the form of studies:
Study in C; Running Dance; Arioso;
The Water Garden; Romance; Boutade;
The Young Willow; Scherzando; Aubade;
Chromatic Waltz; Arpeggione; Processional (1966W)
Three Dances: Mazurka; Pavane; Ländler 1967/68 (1981C)
Three for Two   (1970W) pf 4 hands
Prelude and Toccata   1976 (2000M)
Valse Française   (1980C) also 2pf
Cuckoo Dance   (2000M)
Spring Pastorale   (2000M)
Times Change   (2000M)
Country Dance   (2002M)
Moto perpetuo (study in F min)   (2002M)

Songs ('art' songs)

Name or first line/author/date of composition/(date of publication + publisher)

Ah, how sweet it is to love!   Dryden/1970s/(1994T)
Ballade   Lindsay Kyme/1953/Prowse & Co.
Bay in Anglesey, A   Betjeman/1976/(1980W)
Blind Boy, The   Collie Cibber/c.1960/unp.
Blow, blow thou winter wind   Shakespeare/by 1944/(1949L 1992T)
Business Girls   Betjeman/1976/(1980W)
Cherry Blooming, The   Joseph Ellison/1940s/(1999T)
Come away, come sweet love   anon 16th C/1960s/(1993T)
Come away, death   Shakespeare/by 1944/(1949L 1992T)
Come live with me and be my love   Marlowe/1940s/(2000M)
Crabbed Age and Youth   Shakespeare/1960s/(1992T)
Cuckoo, The   Shakespeare/1960s/(1992T)
Devout Lover, A   Thomas Randolph/1960s/(1993T)
Echoes   T Moore/1960s/(1999T)
Elegy on the death of a mad dog   Goldsmith/1947/unp.
Enchantment, The   Thomas Otway/1960s/(1999T)
Encouragements to a Lover   Sir J Suckling/1950s/(1993T)
Faithless Lover, The   Anon/1960s/(1993T)

Fly, fly you happy shepherds	Vanbrugh/1963/unp.
Frosty Night	M Armstrong/1976/(1985C 1992T)
Holding the Night	M Armstrong/1976/(1985C 1992T)
How sweet I roamed from field to field	Blake/1940s/unp.
I feed a flame within	Dryden/1970s/(1994T)
It was lover and his lass	Shakespeare/c.1944/(1992T)
Knot, The	Campion/1940s/unp.
Love is a sickness	Samuel Daniel/1960s/(1999T)
Love Lyric (who killed the clock)	Joseph Ellison/c1943/unp.
Love was once a little boy	Anon/c.1944/unp.
Love will find out the way	Anon/?/unp.
Mélisande	14th c Fr,Aitken/1950s/(1993T)
My heart is like a singing bird	C Rossetti/1946/unp.
My proper Bess, my pretty Bess	Skelton/1960s/(1993T)
My true love hath my heart	Sir P Sidney/1944/(1999T)
Oh lovely nymph, the world's on fire	Vanbrugh/1963/unp.
Panorama	?/c.1943 /unp.
Parting, The	M Drayton/1960s/(1999T)
Reconcilement, The	Sir J Sheffield/1970s/(1994T)
Separation	M Armstrong/1976/(1985C 1992T)
Sister, awake	Anon/1970s/(1994T)
Slumber Song	Joseph Ellison/1940s/unp.
Snowflakes	Longfellow/1940s/unp.
Song of a Nightclub Proprietress	Betjeman/1976/(1980W)
Take, o take those lips away	Shakespeare/1960s/(1992T)
Thankyou Lord	L.Kyme/?/(1953 Keith Prowse)
This is the time when bit by bit	K T Hinkson/1940s/unp.
Through the Centuries	M Armstrong/1976/(1985C 1992T)
To Daffodils	Herrick/1967/(1992T)
To Music	Herrick/1967/(1992T)
To Phyllis	Herrick/1967/(1992T)
To the Virgins	Herrick/1967/(1992T)
To the Willow Tree	Herrick/1967/(1992T)
Twas on the midmost day in June	J Ellison/c.1943 /unp.
Undenominational	Betjeman/1976/(1980W)
Under the greenwood tree	Shakespeare/by 1944/(1949L 1992T)
Upper Lambourne	Betjeman/1976/(1980W)
Weep you no more, sad fountains	Anon/1950s/(1993T)
What a pother of late	Vanbrugh/1963/unp.
What I fancy, I approve	Herrick/c.1950/(2000M)
When yielding first to Damon's flame	Vanbrugh/1963/unp.
Willow Song	Shakespeare/c.1943 /unp.

The song-sets, as conceived by Dring, are as follows:

3 Shakespeare Songs: Under the greenwood tree; Come away, death; Blow, blow thou winter wind

5 Betjeman Songs: A bay in Anglesey; Business girls; Song of a nightclub proprietress; Undenominational; Upper Lambourne

Love and time: Sister, awake; Ah! How sweet it is to love; I feed a flame; The Reconcilement

Show Songs / Humorous 'Light' Songs

Most of Dring's material for revue is thought to be no longer in existence; we're very lucky to have these few items. If you have any other songs in your possession, *please* get in touch.

A Little Goes a Long Way	(2003M)
Can't you come in softly, Mr Brown	(2004M)
Don't *Play Your Sonata Tonight, Mister Humphries*	(2001M)
Everything Detestable is Best	(2002M)
High in the Pines	(2001M)
I've brought you away	(2000M)
I've Found the Proms	(2001M)
I Should Have Trusted You, Darling	(2002M)
The Model Models	(2002M)
The Principal Boy	(2003M)
Snowman	(2001M)
Spring and Cauli (for RCM)	ms RL
There's Nothing to Stop us Now, Dear	(2002M)
Torch Song	(2004M)

Can't You Come In Softly, Mr Brown!

Darling! We're home now listen to me,
We've got to come in Sh! Quietly
Remember it's late and they can hear every word
In the flat upstairs every sound can be heard,
And don't turn the lights on at this time of night
The switch makes a noise and the light's so bright
It shines right into the flat next door,
And I know they're asleep 'cos I heard them snore – (crash!)

Can't you come in softly, Mister Brown
Can't you go tip-toe Mister Brown
Can't you treat the floor more carefully like a mouse in a public library
Let your feet down lightly Mister Brown
When it's late at nightly, Mister Brown
Use your toes, Mister Brown, lift your heels
You should know which is *me* by the *feel*!
I'm not complaining, I like you big and tall
But quit making love to a twelve foot wall!
The sofa's so cosy The moonlight's on my gown
Come over here and settle down!
Can't you steer over here, Mister Brown Can't you kiss me?
You've missed me Mister Brown
And here I am in the pale moonlight
While you play hide-and-seek all night
Can't you find me Mister Brown?

The people upstairs go to bed at nine-thirty,
they've got two beds right here and here,
So you'll crash around quietly if you love me at all,
There are twelve sets of ears sleeping round these walls
Don't move that chair - the castor squeaks!
Don't go over there – the floorboard creaks!
Don't wake the dead they want to sleep.
I think I will go barmy if you don't stop tumbling
Already I can hear the neighbours gossiping and grumbling
"Don't the Browns make a noise! What *does* that husband do?"

"I don't think the Browns get on"
"What grounds d'you found your news upon?"
"All that bloomin' noise they make – he *beats* her – I heard him –
Kep' me awake –"
"And I saw him THROW things –
I'll complain if it happens *once* again!"

So – can't you come in softly, Mister Brown
Won't you go tip-toe, Mister Brown
Won't you treat the floor more carefully like a mouse in a public library
Let your feet down lightly, Mister Brown
When it's late at nightly, Mister Brown
Use your toes Mister Brown, Lift your heels
You should know which is me by the *feel*!
I'm not complaining, I like you big and tall!
But quite making love to a twelve foot wall!
The sofa's so cosy The moonlight's on my gown
Come over here! And settle down,
Can't you steer over here, Mister Brown
The way is clear, Mister Brown
If you don't kiss me by the count of three,
It's the very last chance you'll get from me!
One!.................(crash!) Two! ………….. (bang!)
Oooh….! Mister Brown!!

Words Charlotte Mitchell, set to music by Madeleine Dring

The drowsy Tidgit. Has strong somnambulistic tendencies and can be heard nightly thudding to the ground.

IDYLL

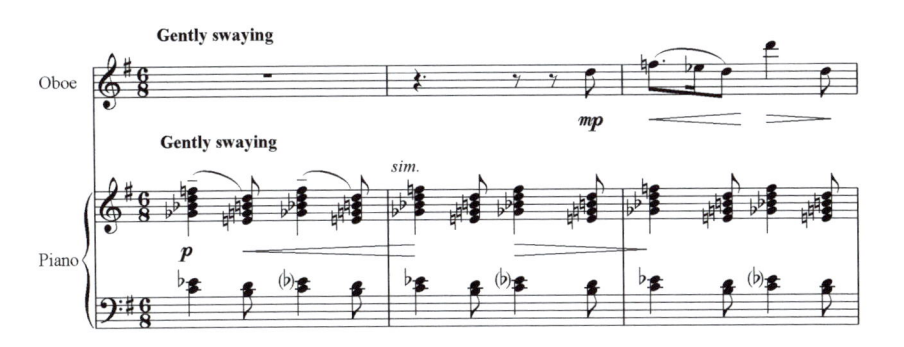

Madeleine Dring

Jubilate

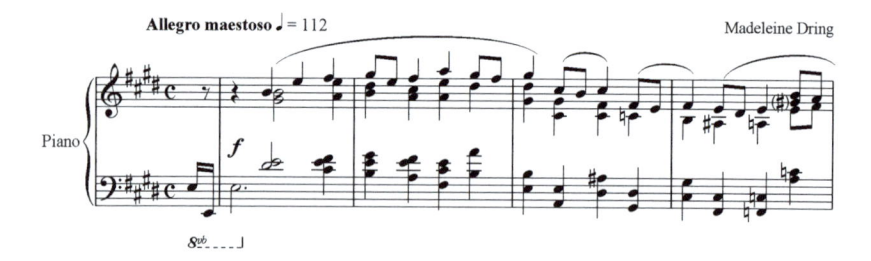

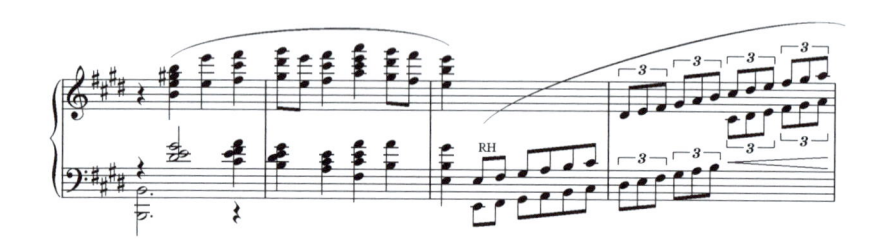

Madeleine Dring

Waltz (with apologies)

What I Fancy I Approve

Words:
Robert Herrick

Music:
Madeleine Dring

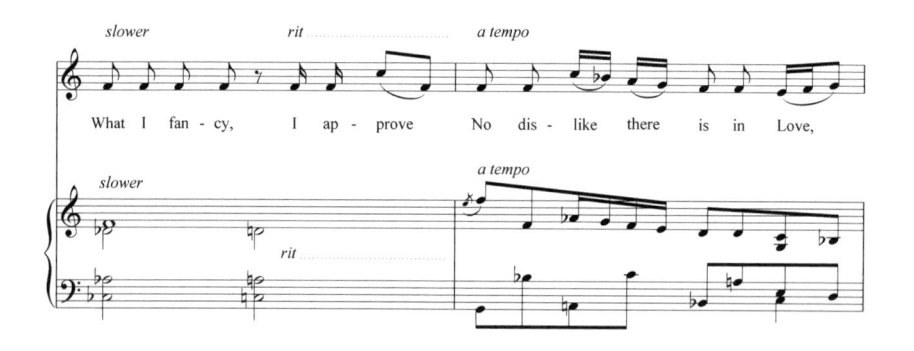

extract from 'High in the Pines' (from *Child's Play*)

Index

A bay in Anglesey 61
A poor soul sat sighing 54
Adrian, Max 18
Ah how sweet it is to love! 60
Airs on a Shoestring 18
Aitken, Dan 16
Allen, Sir Hugh 6
Amis, John 57-8
Apple-Pie Order 41
Armstrong, Michael
    viii,18,28,31,62-4
Arnold, Malcolm 44
Aspinall, Dorothea 6
Babes in the Wood 19
Bailey, John 19
Barne, Betty 6, 9
Bax, Arnold 9
Bennett, William 48
Bergner, Elizabeth 4
Betjeman, John 55, 61-2
Blow, blow thou winter wind 56
Blue Air 61
Bowen, Lance 47
Brister, Wanda 15, 61
Bruch, Max 9
Buck, Sir Percy 6
Bull, E Angela 6, 12-4, 46
Bush, Geoffrey viii, 55
Business Girls 55,61
Can't you come in softly Mister Brown 88-9
Caribbean Dance 43
Centre for Spiritual and
    Psychological Studies
    25, 27,67
Child's Play 19, 52
Coates, Eric 17
Colour Suite 42,61
Come away, come sweet love 54, 58
Come away, death 54, 56, 59
Come let us now resolve 54

Cooper, Kathleen 16
Crabbed Age and Youth 57
Crouch, Doris ix, 4, 29
Cuckoo, The 21, 54, 57
"Cuckoo" Dance 45
Cupboard Love 20, 44
Daniel, Nicholas 47
Danza Gaya 43
Dedications 58-9
Dinn, Freda 6
***Don't** play your sonata tonight, Mister Humphries* 10, 26, 52
Dring, Cecil jnr 2, 15
Dring, Cecil John 2
Dring, Madeleine
    American visits 4, 21
    appearance 3-5
    birth 2
    cartoons 7,26,38,51,66,89
    creativity 35-6
    death 64
    diaries 7,9,11,19,67
    humour 17
    inspiration 27-36
    instrumental music 46-50
    loneliness 11,20,22,31,34
    marriage 15
    performing 7-8,12,32-33
    piano music 39-45
    psychic awareness 1, 7,27-30,36
    reincarnation 4,28
    school 3,11
    songs 52-64
    telepathy 28-9
Dring, Winefride Isabel 2, 15
Emperor and the Nightingale, The 13
Encouragements to a Lover 57
Evans, Jewel 4
Everything Detestable is Best 45
Fair Queen of Wu, The 20

Faithless Lover, The 54, 58
Fantasy Sonata 28, 40-1
Festival Scherzo 17, 44, 47
Fisher, Alistair 53
Five by Ten 44
Florida International Music Festival 22
Fly, Leslie 3, 10,30,40,53
Four Night Songs 62
Frank, Peter 43
Frazer, Moyra 18
Fresh Airs 18
From Here and There 18
Frosty Night 62
Gale, Ursula 12
Gaskell, Lilian 11
Gibbs, C. Armstrong v, vi, 6
Gough Matthews, Michael 28-9
Grainger, Percy 42
Green, Topliss 4
Halstead, Tony 75
Hamburg, Hope 47
Hemmer, Eugene 23, 25, 33-4, 53, 67
High in the pines 52, 94
Hill, Rose viii, 18
Holder, Ray 15
Holding the Night 62
Howells, Herbert vii, 6,12,15, 20, 56,65
I feed a flame 17, 49
Idyll 47, 90
Ireland, John 40
It was a lover 57
Italian Dance 43, 48
I've found the Proms 37-8
Jacob, Gordon 36
Jig 41
Jubilate 45, 91
Jung, Carl 1, 25
Kaplan, Leigh 23, 43
Kenny, Courtney ix, 52, 54
Kensington Gores 19

La Retraite Convent, Clapham Park 11
Ländler 43
Lister, Laurier 18
Live, live with me 54
Lloyd, Peter 23
Lloyd Webber, Dr W 7
Lord, Jeremy Roger ix,15
Lord, Roger Frewen v-ix, 7,15,20,22-23, 28,33,35,47-8, 50,58,63,65
Lord, Simon William ix
Love and Time 23, 59-62
Love is a sickness 54, 61
Maconchy, Elizabeth 44
Marsden, Betty 18
Mazurka 43, 61
Mélisande 58
Merrick, Frank 19
Milhaud, Darius 9
Mitchell, Charlotte iix, 19, 89
Moto Perpetuo 45
Nightfall 44
Pavane 43
Pay the Piper 18
Pennyman, Dorothy 19
Players Theatre 19
Polka (for oboe) 42, 48
Polka (for piano) 17, 40, 42
Poulenc, Francis 41, 55
Previn, André ix, 22-3, 48
Prelude and Toccata (1948) 16
Prelude and Toccata (1976) 44, 65
Prokofiev, Sergei 9
psychometry 21
Purcell, Henry 32
Rachmaninov, Sergei 4, 9, 37,40
Rawsthorne, Alan 17
Real Princess, The 20, 44
Reconcilement, The 60-1
Reed, W. H. 6,47

Romance (for violin) 6, 11, 46
Royal College of Music xii,3-
    14,19,33,35,40,46,53
Rubel, Margaret 6, 19
Rubbra, Edmund 44
St Andrew's Catholic School,
    Streatham 3
Sargent, Malcolm 57
Scales, Prunella ix,19
Separation 62-3
Since there's no help 61
Sister, awake 49, 61
Somebody's Murdered Uncle 16
Sonata for Two Pianos 41
Song of a Nightclub Proprietress
    43, 55, 61
Spring 43-4, 47
Spring and cauli 10, 52
Spring Pastorale 43, 45,47
Steiner, Rudolf 25
Take, O take those lips away 57
Tango ('cello & orch) 47
Tango (oboe) 47
Tarantelle 16, 43
Tass, Peter 4
Tear, Robert 58
Thankyou, Lord 53
Three Piece Suite 50
Three Shakespeare Songs 34,
    53,56
Three Variations on Lilliburlero
    41

Through the Centuries 62-3
Times Change 45
To Daffodils 58
To Music 59
To Phyllis 59
To the Virgins 58
To the Willow Tree 59
Torch Song 50-2
Trio for Flute, Oboe and Piano 23,
    44,48-9
*Trio for Oboe, Bassoon and
    Harpsichord* 44, 49
Trimble, Joan 6
Undenominational 61
Under the greenwood tree 56
Upper Lambourne 49, 61
Vagabond 33,40
Valse Française 43
Vaughan Williams, Ralph vii, 6
Waltz Finale 40
Waltz (for oboe) 48
Waltz (with apologies) 21
Weep you no more, sad fountains
    58
West Indian Dance 43
What I fancy, I approve 17
Who killed the clock 54
Why so pale and wan, fond lover
    54
WIB Waltz 48
Willows 33, 40
Wood, Richard 20, 22

Photographs reproduced by kind permission of Roger Lord.